TORAH PORTIONS WORKBOOK
LEVITICUS

THIS WORKBOOK BELONGS TO:

_____

©2017 TORAH TOWN
Gary A. Arbaugh
Fay A. Arbaugh

Deuteronomy 6:5-9 "Love the Lord your God with all your heart, with all your soul, and with all your strength. Take to heart these words that I give you today. Repeat them to your children. Talk about them when you're at home or away, when you lie down or get up. Write them down, and tie them around your wrist, and wear them as headbands as a reminder. Write them on the door frames of your houses and on your gates."

Deuteronomy 4:9-10 "But watch out! Be careful never to forget what you yourself have seen. Do not let these memories escape from your mind as long as you live! And be sure to pass them on to your children and grandchildren. Never forget the day when you stood before the Lord your God at Mount Sinai, where he told me, Summon the people before me, and I will personally instruct them. Then they will learn to fear me as long as they live, and they will teach their children to fear me also."

Deuteronomy 11:19 Teach them to your children. "Talk about them when you are at home and when you are on the road, when you are going to bed and when you are getting up."

Matthew 19:13-15 "One day some parents brought their children to Yeshua so he could lay his hands on them and pray for them. But the disciples scolded the parents for bothering him. But Yeshua said, "Let the children come to me. Don't stop them! For the Kingdom of Heaven belongs to those who are like these children." And he placed his hands on their heads and blessed them before he left."

Proverbs 20:11 "Even a child makes himself known by his doings, whether his work is pure, and whether it is right."

Proverbs 22:6 "Train up a child in the way he should go: and when he is old, he will not depart from it."

We can all agree that we see things around us changing rapidly as the "end times" are nearing. We see that in order for our children to be spiritually grounded in their faith and able to fight the spiritual battles that lay ahead they need to be prepared.

We would all like to be able to shelter our children from what lies ahead and protect them from all the "bad" around them. But really, if we equip them with God's Word, and teach them the love of Yeshua, what better gift could we give them.

We feel strongly that to **"train up a child in the way he should go..."** they need to be present. They need to hear what the Scriptures say, and feel as if they are a part of the reason that they are going to study. They should also feel comfortable enough that if they desire to participate in a group discussion that they are able. We do understand that getting children involved has it's challenges, and this is not something that happens at one meeting. It takes time and patience on EVERYONES part. Even those who do not have children can help. We are a body of believers and all aspects of that body should be working together as a whole.

FELLOWSHIP LEADERS:

What can you do for your group to help the children want to be more involved?

- Do you give children an opportunity to read (shorter broken down segments) during meeting.
- Do you ask them for assistance in setting up chairs or distributing handouts?
- Can you come up with some more simplistic questions for children to answer during that weeks Torah portion? What was Abraham's sons name? How many of each animal was on the Arc? Etc.
- Is there a child that would like to say a prayer?

THOSE ATTENDING WITHOUT CHILDREN:

- Do you have a listening ear?
- Do you have songs to sing or stories to tell that children would like to hear?
- Could you "adopt" a child for a day? Sit with them, help them to pay attention or to listen?

OTHER SUGGESTIONS:

- **Adults:** Make "deeper" topic notes during the study/bible reading while children are present...once you are finished, excuse the children if they want to then go play or have desert. Everyone takes a short break, then if there are "deeper" things that others would like to discuss you can do that while children are playing. Not everything is child appropriate, so this will offer adults an opportunity to discuss further the scriptures or topics they desire.

- After study, commend the children that participated...tell them what a good job they did with their reading, or how much you liked their comments or prayer.

- **Children/Teens:** Encourage your child to associate with "older" ones attending.

- Encourage your child to get to know those in the group better...ask them questions about when they were kids, how were things different. What are some of their hobbies or interest?

- Is there something your child can do to help those who are elderly? Get them a drink...carry their bags to the car for them. etc.

We realize that there are many different situations and circumstances that parents and grandparents and fellowships deal with regarding this issue and nothing is black and white. Children learn in many different ways, and a 14 year old is not going to have the same interest as a 4 year old, but there are countless ways that we can incorporate our children of all ages to be present during the Bible Study. Some of these may be things you already do, but it may also be a way that we can all work together to help each other in love.

Even if your study currently does things a certain way, maybe you can offer some suggestions to the group or come up with your own ideas or ways to incorporate children into your home study. This may be a little more different than what you have done in the past or are currently doing, but if everyone has the same goal in mind, which is to bring up our children to a deeper understanding and greater knowledge of God's word, then it will be worth it, we will have WON the battle!

Torah Town has put together this booklet as a tool to help Parents, Fellowship Leaders, and even those of the home study family that don't have children. We have tried to incorporate something for all ages and interest. We pray that this will be a blessing to everyone young and old.

And, as always, feel free to make as many copies as you need and share them with others.

To the Parents:

This workbook is designed to enhance your child's learning and participation during Your Community Fellowship Meetings and throughout the week leading up to each Sabbath. In it you will find many activities for each parsha segment, including verses from the Prophets and the New Testament that we pray will both stimulate the mind and keep little hands busy.

You will find each Torah Portion is broken down into daily readings. You may decide on using the Torah Portions in this book as a homeschooling tool. The World English Bible (WEB) is used throughout and we have changed Yahweh to YHWH to allow for your personal interpretation of the Name. We chose this version since it is easily read and can be understood by younger children.

Each Torah Portion has one or more **highlighted text** pertaining to a concept, idea or commandment, and are for spurring thought, verbal interaction and participation.

About Our Activities and Games:

MAKE A MARK – Is a listening game to see how many times someone in the assembly says certain words. This will instill good listening habits along with paying attention to the Torah Reading.

FIRST FIND – This is a Scripture Hunting game that will build knowledge of the location of Bible Books and increase participation in the Bible Study. Allow them to read the passage they find and have a special treat or small gift like scripture pencils to give to whoever finds the passage first.

COLORING PAGE – Each Coloring page is based on the weekly Torah Portion. Allow them to color while listening to the Bible Study. Children are great multi-taskers and you will be surprised at how much they absorb.

WORD FIND – Is the standard word search game where each word is based on the Parsha reading. Aimed at the older children to keep them interested in the topics presented each week.

CROSSWORD – For more advanced or older children. As with all other activities, it is based on the weekly Torah Portion, Prophets or New Testament verses for that week.

VERSE FIND – The letters are scrambled below a grid. The object is to solve in order to know the contents of the verse. (The Answer is Provided in the Title)

SCRAMBLE – Several words are scrambled and in order to solve the puzzle. Once the words are discovered, match the corresponding number with the letter to find the hidden phrase.

HIDDEN VERSE – Solve the hidden verse by finding the words in the list and then copy the remaining letters in order on the lines provided. (The Answer is Provided in the Title)

"Children are great imitators. So give them something great to imitate."

TABLE OF CONTENTS
World English Bible* used throughout
Yahweh changed to YHWH to allow for your personal interpretation of the Name

VAYIKRA (LEVITICUS)

WEEK	PARSHA NAME	ENGLISH	PORTION	PAGE
24	Vayikra וַיִּקְרָא	And He Called	Lev. 1:1 – 6:7*	6
25	Tzav צַו	Command!	Lev. 6:1 - 8:36	19
26	Shemini שְׁמִינִי	Eighth	Lev. 9:1 - 11:47	31
27	Tazria תַזְרִיעַ	She Bears Seed	Lev. 12:1 - 13:59	42
28	Metzora מְצֹרָע	Infected One	Lev. 14:1 - 15:33	52
29	Archarei Mot אַחֲרֵי מוֹת	After The Death	Lev. 16:1 - 18:30	65
30	Kedoshim קְדֹשִׁים	Holy Ones	Lev. 19:1 - 20:27	76
31	Emor אֱמֹר	Say Gently	Lev. 21:1 - 24:23	86
32	Behar בְּהַר	On The Mount	Lev. 25:1 - 26:2	100
33	Bechukotai בְּחֻקֹּתַי	In My Statutes	Lev. 26:3 - 27:34	110

* The Hebrew Bible and the Complete Jewish Bible (CJB) lists Vayikra portion as Lev. 1:1–5:26, however Leviticus 5:19 is the last verse in most other translations and is continued in Chapter 6.

** One week is always Passover and another is always Sukkot, and the final parashah, *V'Zot HaBerachah*, is always read on Simchat Torah. Therefore, there can be up to 53 weeks available for the other 53 portions. In years with fewer than 53 available weeks, some readings are combined to achieve the needed number of weekly readings. **

VAYIKRA

וַיִּקְרָא

LEVITICUS

It Means: **And He Called**

Our Twenty-Forth Torah Portion is called Vayikra! וַיִּקְרָא

Leviticus 1:1 – Leviticus 6:7

PROPHETS: Isaiah 43:21-44:23; 66
NEW TESTAMENT: Romans 8:1-13; Hebrews 10:1-39; 13:10-16

MAKE A MARK

Each time you hear someone say one of the words below make a "/" beside the word. See how many marks you can get!

salt	
guilty	
priest	
blood	
Aaron	
altar	

FIRST FIND

~

If someone mentions a verse or scripture that is NOT in this Torah Portion, see if YOU can be the First to Find it!

VAYIKRA

```
S B A I F F P N X F X Q C S
G W M E C A O R L O T B T T
N G O O C R T O I R U I M A
I O R S A I U R E E U K S B
R A A A T R F S A R S W E E
E T N A E A P I F T O T S R
F S G C P A T T R O L B O N
F J N F S E S U D C I A M A
O E I S I R E B T R A P V C
Y S S G I R L H D E E S A L
H A A F C O E S S E A P V E
W L E T O A T O N E M E N T
H T L D H Y H B U R N T J V
Y V P J I U A P I S R A E L
```

AARON	FIRSTFRUITS	SACRIFICE
ALTAR	FLOUR	SALT
ATONEMENT	GOATS	SHEEP
BIRDS	ISRAEL	STATUTE
BLOOD	MOSES	TABERNACLE
BURNT	OFFERINGS	TRESPASS
FAT	PLEASING AROMA	WOOD
FIRE	PRIEST	YHWH

Word Search Created by Torah Town

LEVITICUS 1:2
Speak to the children of Israel, and tell them, 'When anyone of you offers an offering to YHWH, you shall offer your offering of the livestock, from the herd and from the flock.

Laws for Burnt Offerings

SUNDAY Lev 1:1 *YHWH called to Moses, and spoke to him from the Tent of Meeting*, saying,

Lev 1:2 "Speak to the children of Israel, and tell them, 'When anyone of you offers an offering to YHWH, you shall offer your offering of the livestock, from the herd and from the flock.

Lev 1:3 "'If his offering is a burnt offering from the herd, he shall offer a male without defect. He shall offer it at the door of the Tent of Meeting, that he may be accepted before YHWH.

Lev 1:4 He shall lay his hand on the head of the burnt offering, and it shall be accepted for him to make atonement for him.

Lev 1:5 He shall kill the bull before YHWH. Aaron's sons, the priests, shall present the blood and sprinkle the blood around on the altar that is at the door of the Tent of Meeting.

Lev 1:6 He shall flay the burnt offering, and cut it into pieces.

Lev 1:7 The sons of Aaron the priest shall put fire on the altar, and lay wood in order on the fire;

Lev 1:8 and Aaron's sons, the priests, shall lay the pieces, the head, and the fat in order on the wood that is on the fire which is on the altar;

Lev 1:9 but its innards and its legs he shall wash with water. The priest shall burn all of it on the altar, for a burnt offering, an offering made by fire, of a pleasant aroma to YHWH.

Lev 1:10 "'If his offering is from the flock, from the sheep, or from the goats, for a burnt offering, he shall offer a male without defect.

Lev 1:11 He shall kill it on the north side of the altar before YHWH. Aaron's sons, the priests, shall sprinkle its blood around on the altar.

Lev 1:12 He shall cut it into its pieces, with its head and its fat. The priest shall lay them in order on the wood that is on the fire which is on the altar,

Lev 1:13 but the innards and the legs he shall wash with water. The priest shall offer the whole, and burn it on the altar. It is a burnt offering, an offering made by fire, of a pleasant aroma to YHWH.

MONDAY Lev 1:14 "'If his offering to YHWH is a burnt offering of birds, then he shall offer his offering of turtledoves or of young pigeons.

Lev 1:15 The priest shall bring it to the altar, and wring off its head, and burn it on the altar; and its blood shall be drained out on the side of the altar;

Lev 1:16 and he shall take away its crop with its filth, and cast it beside the altar on the east part, in the place of the ashes.

Lev 1:17 He shall tear it by its wings, but shall not divide it apart. The priest shall burn it on the altar, on the wood that is on the fire. *It is a burnt offering, an offering made by fire, of a pleasant aroma to YHWH.*

Laws for Grain Offerings

Lev 2:1 "'When anyone offers an offering of a meal offering to YHWH, his offering shall be of fine flour. He shall pour oil on it, and put frankincense on it.

Lev 2:2 He shall bring it to Aaron's sons, the priests; and he shall take his handful of its fine flour, and of its oil, with all its frankincense; and the priest shall burn its memorial on the altar, an offering made by fire, of a pleasant aroma to YHWH.

Lev 2:3 That which is left of the meal offering shall be Aaron's and his sons'. It is a most holy thing of the offerings of YHWH made by fire.

Lev 2:4 "'When you offer an offering of a meal offering baked in the oven, it shall be unleavened cakes of fine flour mixed with oil, or unleavened wafers anointed with oil.

Lev 2:5 If your offering is a meal offering made on a griddle, it shall be of unleavened fine flour, mixed with oil.

Lev 2:6 You shall cut it in pieces, and pour oil on it. It is a meal offering.

TUESDAY Lev 2:7 If your offering is a meal offering of the pan, it shall be made of fine flour with oil.

Lev 2:8 You shall bring the meal offering that is made of these things to YHWH: and it shall be presented to the priest, and he shall bring it to the altar.

Lev 2:9 The priest shall take from the meal offering its memorial, and shall burn it on the altar, an offering made by fire, of a pleasant aroma to YHWH.

Lev 2:10 That which is left of the meal offering shall be Aaron's and his sons'. It is a thing most holy of the offerings of YHWH made by fire.

Lev 2:11 "'No meal offering, which you shall offer to YHWH, shall be made with yeast; for you shall burn no yeast, nor any honey, as an offering made by fire to YHWH.

Lev 2:12 *As an offering of first fruits you shall offer them to YHWH: but they shall not rise up for a pleasant aroma on the altar.*

Lev 2:13 Every offering of your meal offering you shall season with salt. You shall not allow the salt of the covenant of your God to be lacking from your meal offering. With all your offerings you shall offer salt.

Lev 2:14 "'If you offer a meal offering of first fruits to YHWH, you shall offer for the meal offering of your first fruits grain in the ear parched with fire, bruised grain of the fresh ear.

Lev 2:15 You shall put oil on it, and lay frankincense on it: it is a meal offering.

Lev 2:16 The priest shall burn as its memorial, part of its bruised grain, and part of its oil, along with all its frankincense: it is an offering made by fire to YHWH.

Laws for Peace Offerings

WEDNESDAY Lev 3:1 "'If his offering is a sacrifice of peace offerings; if he offers it from the herd, whether male or female, he shall offer it without defect before YHWH.

Lev 3:2 He shall lay his hand on the head of his offering, and kill it at the door of the Tent of Meeting: and Aaron's sons, the priests, shall sprinkle the blood around on the altar.

Lev 3:3 He shall offer of the sacrifice of peace offerings an offering made by fire to YHWH; the fat that covers the innards, and all the fat that is on the innards,

Lev 3:4 and the two kidneys, and the fat that is on them, which is by the loins, and the cover on the liver, with the kidneys, he shall take away.

Lev 3:5 Aaron's sons shall burn it on the altar on the burnt offering, which is on the wood that is on the fire: it is an offering made by fire, of a pleasant aroma to YHWH.

Lev 3:6 "'If his offering for a sacrifice of peace offerings to YHWH is from the flock; male or female, he shall offer it without defect.

Lev 3:7 *If he offers a lamb for his offering, then he shall offer it before YHWH;*

Lev 3:8 and he shall lay his hand on the head of his offering, and kill it before the Tent of Meeting: and Aaron's sons shall sprinkle its blood around on the altar.

Lev 3:9 He shall offer from the sacrifice of peace offerings an offering made by fire to YHWH; its fat, the entire tail fat, he shall take away close to the backbone; and the fat that covers the inwards, and all the fat that is on the inwards,

Lev 3:10 and the two kidneys, and the fat that is on them, which is by the loins, and the cover on the liver, with the kidneys, he shall take away.

Lev 3:11 The priest shall burn it on the altar: it is the food of the offering made by fire to YHWH.

Lev 3:12 "'If his offering is a goat, then he shall offer it before YHWH:

Lev 3:13 and he shall lay his hand on its head, and kill it before the Tent of Meeting; and the sons of Aaron shall sprinkle its blood around on the altar.

Lev 3:14 He shall offer from it as his offering, an offering made by fire to YHWH; the fat that covers the innards, and all the fat that is on the innards,

Lev 3:15 and the two kidneys, and the fat that is on them, which is by the loins, and the cover on the liver, with the kidneys, he shall take away.

Lev 3:16 The priest shall burn them on the altar: it is the food of the offering made by fire, for a pleasant aroma; all the fat is YHWH's.

Lev 3:17 *"'It shall be a perpetual statute throughout your generations in all your dwellings, that you shall eat neither fat nor blood.'"*

Laws for Sin Offerings

THURSDAY Lev 4:1 YHWH spoke to Moses, saying,

Lev 4:2 "Speak to the children of Israel, saying, 'If anyone sins unintentionally, in any of the things which YHWH has commanded not to be done, and does any one of them:

Lev 4:3 if the anointed priest sins so as to bring guilt on the people, then let him offer for his sin, which he has sinned, a young bull without defect to YHWH for a sin offering.

Lev 4:4 He shall bring the bull to the door of the Tent of Meeting before YHWH; and he shall lay his hand on the head of the bull, and kill the bull before YHWH.

Lev 4:5 The anointed priest shall take some of the blood of the bull, and bring it to the Tent of Meeting.

Lev 4:6 The priest shall dip his finger in the blood, and sprinkle some of the blood seven times before YHWH, before the veil of the sanctuary.

Lev 4:7 The priest shall put some of the blood on the horns of the altar of sweet incense before YHWH, which is in the Tent of Meeting; and he shall pour out all of rest of the blood of the bull at the base of the altar of burnt offering, which is at the door of the Tent of Meeting.

Lev 4:8 He shall take all the fat of the bull of the sin offering from it; the fat that covers the innards, and all the fat that is on the innards,

Lev 4:9 and the two kidneys, and the fat that is on them, which is by the loins, and the cover on the liver, with the kidneys, he shall take away,

Lev 4:10 as it is taken from the bull of the sacrifice of peace offerings. The priest shall burn them on the altar of burnt offering.

Lev 4:11 The bull's skin, all its meat, with its head, and with its legs, its innards, and its dung,

Lev 4:12 **he shall carry the whole bull outside of the camp to a clean place, where the ashes are poured out, and burn it on wood with fire. Where the ashes are poured out, it shall be burned.**

Lev 4:13 "'If the whole congregation of Israel sins, and the thing is hidden from the eyes of the assembly, and they have done any of the things which YHWH has commanded not to be done, and are guilty;

Lev 4:14 when the sin in which they have sinned is known, then the assembly shall offer a young bull for a sin offering, and bring it before the Tent of Meeting.

Lev 4:15 The elders of the congregation shall lay their hands on the head of the bull before YHWH; and the bull shall be killed before YHWH.

Lev 4:16 The anointed priest shall bring some of the blood of the bull to the Tent of Meeting:

Lev 4:17 and the priest shall dip his finger in the blood, and sprinkle it seven times before YHWH, before the veil.

Lev 4:18 He shall put some of the blood on the horns of the altar which is before YHWH, that is in the Tent of Meeting; and the rest of the blood he shall pour out at the base of the altar of burnt offering, which is at the door of the Tent of Meeting.

Lev 4:19 All its fat he shall take from it, and burn it on the altar.

Lev 4:20 Thus shall he do with the bull; as he did with the bull of the sin offering, so shall he do with this; and the priest shall make atonement for them, and they shall be forgiven.

Lev 4:21 He shall carry the bull outside the camp, and burn it as he burned the first bull. It is the sin offering for the assembly.

Lev 4:22 "'When a ruler sins, and unwittingly does any one of all the things which YHWH his God has commanded not to be done, and is guilty;

Lev 4:23 if his sin, in which he has sinned, is made known to him, he shall bring as his offering a goat, a male without defect.

Lev 4:24 He shall lay his hand on the head of the goat, and kill it in the place where they kill the burnt offering before YHWH. It is a sin offering.

Lev 4:25 The priest shall take some of the blood of the sin offering with his finger, and put it on the horns of the altar of burnt offering. He shall pour out the rest of its blood at the base of the altar of burnt offering.

Lev 4:26 All its fat he shall burn on the altar, like the fat of the sacrifice of peace offerings; and the priest shall make atonement for him concerning his sin, and he will be forgiven.

FRIDAY Lev 4:27 "'If anyone of the common people sins unwittingly, in doing any of the things which YHWH has commanded not to be done, and is guilty;

Lev 4:28 if his sin, which he has sinned, is made known to him, then he shall bring for his offering a goat, a female without defect, for his sin which he has sinned.

Lev 4:29 He shall lay his hand on the head of the sin offering, and kill the sin offering in the place of burnt offering.

Lev 4:30 The priest shall take some of its blood with his finger, and put it on the horns of the altar of burnt offering; and the rest of its blood he shall pour out at the base of the altar.

Lev 4:31 All its fat he shall take away, like the fat is taken away from the sacrifice of peace offerings; and the priest shall burn it on the altar for a pleasant aroma to YHWH; and the priest shall make atonement for him, and he will be forgiven.

Lev 4:32 "'If he brings a lamb as his offering for a sin offering, he shall bring a female without defect.

Lev 4:33 He shall lay his hand on the head of the sin offering, and kill it for a sin offering in the place where they kill the burnt offering.

Lev 4:34 The priest shall take some of the blood of the sin offering with his finger, and put it on the horns of the altar of burnt offering; and all the rest of its blood he shall pour out at the base of the altar.

Lev 4:35 All its fat he shall take away, like the fat of the lamb is taken away from the sacrifice of peace offerings; and the priest shall burn them on the altar, on the offerings of YHWH made by fire; and the priest shall make atonement for him concerning his sin that he has sinned, and he will be forgiven.

Lev 5:1 "'If anyone sins, in that he hears the voice of adjuration, he being a witness, whether he has seen or known, if he doesn't report it, then he shall bear his iniquity.

MY NOTES

Lev 5:2 "'Or if anyone touches any unclean thing, whether it is the carcass of an unclean animal, or the carcass of unclean livestock, or the carcass of unclean creeping things, and it is hidden from him, and he is unclean, then he shall be guilty.

Lev 5:3 "'Or if he touches the uncleanness of man, whatever his uncleanness is with which he is unclean, and it is hidden from him; when he knows of it, then he shall be guilty.

Lev 5:4 "'Or if anyone swears rashly with his lips to do evil, or to do good, whatever it is that a man might utter rashly with an oath, and it is hidden from him; when he knows of it, then he shall be guilty of one of these.

Lev 5:5 **It shall be, when he is guilty of one of these, he shall confess that in which he has sinned:**

Lev 5:6 and he shall bring his trespass offering to YHWH for his sin which he has sinned, a female from the flock, a lamb or a goat, for a sin offering; and the priest shall make atonement for him concerning his sin.

Lev 5:7 "'If he can't afford a lamb, then he shall bring his trespass offering for that in which he has sinned, two turtledoves, or two young pigeons, to YHWH; one for a sin offering, and the other for a burnt offering.

Lev 5:8 He shall bring them to the priest, who shall first offer the one which is for the sin offering, and wring off its head from its neck, but shall not sever it completely.

Lev 5:9 He shall sprinkle some of the blood of the sin offering on the side of the altar; and the rest of the blood shall be drained out at the base of the altar. It is a sin offering.

Lev 5:10 He shall offer the second for a burnt offering, according to the ordinance; and the priest shall make atonement for him concerning his sin which he has sinned, and he shall be forgiven.

SABBATH Lev 5:11 "'But if he can't afford two turtledoves, or two young pigeons, then he shall bring his offering for that in which he has sinned, one tenth of an ephah of fine flour for a sin offering. He shall put no oil on it, and he shall not put any frankincense on it, for it is a sin offering.

Lev 5:12 He shall bring it to the priest, and the priest shall take his handful of it as the memorial portion, and burn it on the altar, on the offerings of YHWH made by fire. It is a sin offering.

Lev 5:13 The priest shall make atonement for him concerning his sin that he has sinned in any of these things, and he will be forgiven; and the rest shall be the priest's, as the meal offering.'"

page 16

Laws for Guilt Offerings

Lev 5:14 YHWH spoke to Moses, saying,

Lev 5:15 "If anyone commits a trespass, and sins unwittingly, in the holy things of YHWH; then he shall bring his trespass offering to YHWH, a ram without defect from the flock, according to your estimation in silver by shekels, after the shekel of the sanctuary, for a trespass offering.

Lev 5:16 He shall make restitution for that which he has done wrong in the holy thing, and shall add a fifth part to it, and give it to the priest; and the priest shall make atonement for him with the ram of the trespass offering, and he will be forgiven.

Lev 5:17 *"If anyone sins, and does any of the things which YHWH has commanded not to be done; though he didn't know it, yet he is guilty, and shall bear his iniquity.*

Lev 5:18 He shall bring a ram without defect from of the flock, according to your estimation, for a trespass offering, to the priest; and the priest shall make atonement for him concerning the thing in which he sinned and didn't know it, and he will be forgiven.

Lev 5:19 It is a trespass offering. He is certainly guilty before YHWH."

Lev 6:1 YHWH spoke to Moses, saying,

Lev 6:2 "If anyone sins, and commits a trespass against YHWH, and deals falsely with his neighbor in a matter of deposit, or of bargain, or of robbery, or has oppressed his neighbor,

Lev 6:3 or has found that which was lost, and dealt falsely therein, and swearing to a lie; in any of these things that a man does, sinning therein;

Lev 6:4 then it shall be, if he has sinned, and is guilty, he shall restore that which he took by robbery, or the thing which he has gotten by oppression, or the deposit which was committed to him, or the lost thing which he found,

Lev 6:5 or any thing about which he has sworn falsely; he shall restore it even in full, and shall add a fifth part more to it. He shall return it to him to whom it belongs in the day of his being found guilty.

Lev 6:6 He shall bring his trespass offering to YHWH, a ram without defect from the flock, according to your estimation, for a trespass offering, to the priest.

Lev 6:7 The priest shall make atonement for him before YHWH, and he will be forgiven concerning whatever he does to become guilty."

VERSE FIND – ROMANS 8:3

```
              O       R
      A       O       N
      H       N   S I       H T
   A I S  G W K A  S I   N H
   U L S E S T W D F T S I H   T L A T L E
   E E N N E S N H O D I H N F U N T W H E
 F O C S D D D O A D L E H T N U I E A D E G
 L L K H F O W E O F D S S I N I S H N F H I S
 C I W O N N R M F E R T O D N E G L E T I N T H
```

HIDDEN VERSE – HEBREWS 10:12

```
S A B U T H E W H B D E N H E
H S U A D O F F I E L T R E R
D O E H N E S B A C I A R I O
F R I N S C L E F O U B R S N
I S A N R E S F S O B E R E O
V E H M R E Y S P W E R B E H
E E S E M A D T I D V N O N W
N O N O E A T L R H R A E O R
I G S H A P E T I H E C A T N
S E D R H T U R T W S L O S F
S H O S A N C T I F I E D K O
F N A P R I E S T F G O D R L
U K Y D T A O G F E S X C O L
D H K B O W M W S D N F L W O
E N O G Y W P N T Q Z T H Y W
```

AARON	GOAT	PRIEST	SHADOW	TENT
BIBLE	GONE	RAM	SHEEP	TRUTH
BUILD	HEBREW	SANCTIFIED	SPIRIT	WILDERNESS
FIRE	HONOR	SEE	STONE	WORK
FOLLOW	MOSES	SERVE	TABERNACLE	YESHUA

___ ___ , _____ ___ ___ ___ _____

_____ ___ _____ ___ _____ , _____ _____ ___ __

__ _____ ___ ___ ____

page 18

TZAV

LEVITICUS

It Means: **COMMAND!**

Our Twenty-Fifth Torah Portion is called Tzav!
Leviticus 6:8 – Leviticus 8:36

PROPHETS: Jeremiah 7:21-8:3; 9:23-24; Malachi 3:1-4:6
NEW TESTAMENT: Matthew 3:11-12; 5:17-19; 7:21-23; 22:10-14; Mark 12:28-34; Romans 8:1-13, 12:1-2; 1 Corinthians 3:9-23; 10:14-23; 1 Timothy 2:1-10; Hebrews 7:23-8:6, 13:10-16; Revelation 6:9-11; 8:1-9:21; 14:6-7; 16:15; 19:6-8

MAKE A MARK

Each time you hear someone say one of the words below make a '/" beside the word. See how many marks you can get!

yeast	
leavening	
sin	
thigh	
temple	
Moses	

FIRST FIND

~

If someone mentions a verse or scripture that is NOT in this Torah Portion, see if YOU can be the First to Find it!

TZAV

```
N S G N I V I G S K N A H T
O O N F V G A R M E N T S D
I N O D E L K N I R P S E E
T S I I C O M M A N D N T C
A P T G L Y E A S T E A H F
N O A L T H I G H V L I P W
I R R E D A M L A P L E I H
M T C S F H A E T D T L J R
O I E S J E L S R L N B I B
B O S E M G A E M A S M E R
A N N V L E N S S M I E C O
E K O N R N V L I I N S A N
W R C B E P H A H N A S E Z
A N O I N T E D R A I A P E
```

ABOMINATION	CONSECRATION	SIN
ANIMAL	EPHAH	SINAI
ANOINTED	GARMENTS	SONS
ASSEMBLE	LEAVENED	SPRINKLED
BREASTPLATE	MEAL	THANKSGIVING
BRONZE	OIL	THIGH
CHILDREN	PEACE	VESSEL
COMMAND	PORTION	YEAST

Word Search Created by Torah Town

LEVITICUS 4:25

The priest shall take some of the blood of the sin offering with his finger, and put it on the horns of the altar of burnt offering. He shall pour out the rest of its blood at the base of the altar of burnt offering.

The Priests and the Offerings

<u>SUNDAY</u> Lev 6:8 YHWH spoke to Moses, saying,

Lev 6:9 "Command Aaron and his sons, saying, 'This is the law of the burnt offering: the burnt offering shall be on the hearth on the altar all night until the morning; and the fire of the altar shall be kept burning on it.

Lev 6:10 The priest shall put on his linen garment, and he shall put on his linen breeches upon his body; and he shall remove the ashes from where the fire has consumed the burnt offering on the altar, and he shall put them beside the altar.

Lev 6:11 *He shall take off his garments, and put on other garments, and carry the ashes outside the camp to a clean place.*

<u>MONDAY</u> Lev 6:12 The fire on the altar shall be kept burning on it, it shall not go out; and the priest shall burn wood on it every morning: and he shall lay the burnt offering in order upon it, and shall burn on it the fat of the peace offerings.

Lev 6:13 *Fire shall be kept burning on the altar continually; it shall not go out.*

Lev 6:14 "'This is the law of the meal offering: the sons of Aaron shall offer it before YHWH, before the altar.

Lev 6:15 He shall take from there his handful of the fine flour of the meal offering, and of its oil, and all the frankincense which is on the meal offering, and shall burn it on the altar for a pleasant aroma, as its memorial, to YHWH.

Lev 6:16 That which is left of it Aaron and his sons shall eat. It shall be eaten without yeast in a holy place. They shall eat it in the court of the Tent of Meeting.

Lev 6:17 It shall not be baked with yeast. I have given it as their portion of my offerings made by fire. It is most holy, as the sin offering, and as the trespass offering.

Lev 6:18 Every male among the children of Aaron shall eat of it, as their portion forever throughout your generations, from the offerings of YHWH made by fire. Whoever touches them shall be holy.'"

Lev 6:19 YHWH spoke to Moses, saying,

Lev 6:20 "This is the offering of Aaron and of his sons, which they shall offer to YHWH in the day when he is anointed: one tenth of an ephah of fine flour for a meal offering perpetually, half of it in the morning, and half of it in the evening.

Lev 6:21 It shall be made with oil in a griddle. When it is soaked, you shall bring it in. You shall offer the meal offering in baked pieces for a pleasant aroma to YHWH.

Lev 6:22 The anointed priest that will be in his place from among his sons shall offer it. By a statute forever, it shall be wholly burned to YHWH.

Lev 6:23 **Every meal offering of a priest shall be wholly burned. It shall not be eaten."**

Lev 6:24 YHWH spoke to Moses, saying,

Lev 6:25 "Speak to Aaron and to his sons, saying, 'This is the law of the sin offering: in the place where the burnt offering is killed, the sin offering shall be killed before YHWH. It is most holy.

Lev 6:26 The priest who offers it for sin shall eat it. It shall be eaten in a holy place, in the court of the Tent of Meeting.

Lev 6:27 Whatever shall touch its flesh shall be holy. When there is any of its blood sprinkled on a garment, you shall wash that on which it was sprinkled in a holy place.

Lev 6:28 But the earthen vessel in which it is boiled shall be broken; and if it is boiled in a bronze vessel, it shall be scoured, and rinsed in water.

Lev 6:29 Every male among the priests shall eat of it: it is most holy.

Lev 6:30 No sin offering, of which any of the blood is brought into the Tent of Meeting to make atonement in the Holy Place, shall be eaten: it shall be burned with fire.

Lev 7:1 "'This is the law of the trespass offering. It is most holy.

Lev 7:2 In the place where they kill the burnt offering, he shall kill the trespass offering; and its blood he shall sprinkle around on the altar.

Lev 7:3 He shall offer all of its fat: the fat tail, and the fat that covers the innards,

Lev 7:4 and the two kidneys, and the fat that is on them, which is by the loins, and the cover on the liver, with the kidneys, shall he take away;

Lev 7:5 and the priest shall burn them on the altar for an offering made by fire to YHWH: it is a trespass offering.

Lev 7:6 **Every male among the priests may eat of it. It shall be eaten in a holy place. It is most holy.**

Lev 7:7 "'As is the sin offering, so is the trespass offering; there is one law for them. The priest who makes atonement with them shall have it.

Lev 7:8 The priest who offers any man's burnt offering, even the priest shall have for himself the skin of the burnt offering which he has offered.

Lev 7:9 Every meal offering that is baked in the oven, and all that is dressed in the pan, and on the griddle, shall be the priest's who offers it.

Lev 7:10 Every meal offering, mixed with oil or dry, belongs to all the sons of Aaron, one as well as another.

TUESDAY Lev 7:11 "'This is the law of the sacrifice of peace offerings, which one shall offer to YHWH.

Lev 7:12 If he offers it for a thanksgiving, then he shall offer with the sacrifice of thanksgiving unleavened cakes mixed with oil, and unleavened wafers anointed with oil, and cakes mixed with oil.

Lev 7:13 With cakes of leavened bread he shall offer his offering with the sacrifice of his peace offerings for thanksgiving.

Lev 7:14 Of it he shall offer one out of each offering for a heave offering to YHWH. It shall be the priest's who sprinkles the blood of the peace offerings.

Lev 7:15 The flesh of the sacrifice of his peace offerings for thanksgiving shall be eaten on the day of his offering. He shall not leave any of it until the morning.

Lev 7:16 "'But if the sacrifice of his offering is a vow, or a freewill offering, it shall be eaten on the day that he offers his sacrifice; and on the next day what remains of it shall be eaten:

Lev 7:17 but what remains of the meat of the sacrifice on the third day shall be burned with fire.

Lev 7:18 If any of the meat of the sacrifice of his peace offerings is eaten on the third day, it will not be accepted, and it shall not be credited to him who offers it. It will be an abomination, and the soul who eats any of it will bear his iniquity.

Lev 7:19 **"'The meat that touches any unclean thing shall not be eaten. It shall be burned with fire. As for the meat, everyone who is clean may eat it;**

Lev 7:20 but the soul who eats of the meat of the sacrifice of peace offerings, that belongs to YHWH, having his uncleanness on him, that soul shall be cut off from his people.

Lev 7:21 When anyone touches any unclean thing, the uncleanness of man, or an unclean animal, or any unclean abomination, and eats some of the meat of the sacrifice of peace offerings, which belong to YHWH, that soul shall be cut off from his people.'"

Lev 7:22 YHWH spoke to Moses, saying,

Lev 7:23 "Speak to the children of Israel, saying, 'You shall eat no fat, of bull, or sheep, or goat.

MY NOTES

Lev 7:24 The fat of that which dies of itself, and the fat of that which is torn of animals, may be used for any other service, but you shall in no way eat of it.

Lev 7:25 For whoever eats the fat of the animal, of which men offer an offering made by fire to YHWH, even the soul who eats it shall be cut off from his people.

Lev 7:26 **You shall not eat any blood, whether it is of bird or of animal, in any of your dwellings.**

Lev 7:27 Whoever it is who eats any blood, that soul shall be cut off from his people.'"

Lev 7:28 YHWH spoke to Moses, saying,

Lev 7:29 "Speak to the children of Israel, saying, 'He who offers the sacrifice of his peace offerings to YHWH shall bring his offering to YHWH out of the sacrifice of his peace offerings.

Lev 7:30 With his own hands he shall bring the offerings of YHWH made by fire. He shall bring the fat with the breast, that the breast may be waved for a wave offering before YHWH.

Lev 7:31 The priest shall burn the fat on the altar, but the breast shall be Aaron's and his sons'.

Lev 7:32 The right thigh you shall give to the priest for a heave offering out of the sacrifices of your peace offerings.

Lev 7:33 He among the sons of Aaron who offers the blood of the peace offerings, and the fat, shall have the right thigh for a portion.

Lev 7:34 For the waved breast and the heaved thigh I have taken from the children of Israel out of the sacrifices of their peace offerings, and have given them to Aaron the priest and to his sons as their portion forever from the children of Israel.'"

Lev 7:35 This is the anointing portion of Aaron, and the anointing portion of his sons, out of the offerings of YHWH made by fire, in the day when he presented them to minister to YHWH in the priest's office;

Lev 7:36 which YHWH commanded to be given them of the children of Israel, in the day that he anointed them. It is their portion forever throughout their generations.

Lev 7:37 This is the law of the burnt offering, of the meal offering, and of the sin offering, and of the trespass offering, and of the consecration, and of the sacrifice of peace offerings;

Lev 7:38 which YHWH commanded Moses in Mount Sinai, in the day that he commanded the children of Israel to offer their offerings to YHWH, in the wilderness of Sinai.

MY NOTES

Consecration of Aaron and His Sons

WEDNESDAY Lev 8:1 YHWH spoke to Moses, saying,

Lev 8:2 "Take Aaron and his sons with him, and the garments, and the anointing oil, and the bull of the sin offering, and the two rams, and the basket of unleavened bread;

Lev 8:3 and assemble all the congregation at the door of the Tent of Meeting."

Lev 8:4 Moses did as YHWH commanded him; and the congregation was assembled at the door of the Tent of Meeting.

Lev 8:5 **Moses said to the congregation, "This is the thing which YHWH has commanded to be done."**

Lev 8:6 Moses brought Aaron and his sons, and washed them with water.

Lev 8:7 He put the coat on him, tied the sash on him, clothed him with the robe, put the ephod on him, and he tied the skillfully woven band of the ephod on him, and fastened it to him with it.

Lev 8:8 He placed the breastplate on him; and in the breastplate he put the Urim and the Thummim.

Lev 8:9 He set the turban on his head; and on the turban, in front, he set the golden plate, the holy crown; as YHWH commanded Moses.

Lev 8:10 Moses took the anointing oil, and anointed the tabernacle and all that was in it, and sanctified them.

Lev 8:11 He sprinkled it on the altar seven times, and anointed the altar and all its vessels, and the basin and its base, to sanctify them.

Lev 8:12 He poured some of the anointing oil on Aaron's head, and anointed him, to sanctify him.

Lev 8:13 Moses brought Aaron's sons, and clothed them with coats, and tied sashes on them, and put headbands on them; as YHWH commanded Moses.

THURSDAY Lev 8:14 He brought the bull of the sin offering, and Aaron and his sons laid their hands on the head of the bull of the sin offering.

Lev 8:15 He killed it; and Moses took the blood, and put it around on the horns of the altar with his finger, and purified the altar, and poured out the blood at the base of the altar, and sanctified it, to make atonement for it.

Lev 8:16 He took all the fat that was on the innards, and the cover of the liver, and the two kidneys, and their fat; and Moses burned it on the altar.

Lev 8:17 **But the bull, and its skin, and its meat, and its dung, he burned with fire outside the camp; as YHWH commanded Moses.**

Lev 8:18 He presented the ram of the burnt offering: and Aaron and his sons laid their hands on the head of the ram.

Lev 8:19 He killed it; and Moses sprinkled the blood around on the altar.

Lev 8:20 He cut the ram into its pieces; and Moses burned the head, and the pieces, and the fat.

Lev 8:21 He washed the innards and the legs with water; and Moses burned the whole ram on the altar. It was a burnt offering for a pleasant aroma. It was an offering made by fire to YHWH; as YHWH commanded Moses.

FRIDAY Lev 8:22 He presented the other ram, the ram of consecration: and Aaron and his sons laid their hands on the head of the ram.

Lev 8:23 He killed it; and Moses took some of its blood, and put it on the tip of Aaron's right ear, and on the thumb of his right hand, and on the great toe of his right foot.

Lev 8:24 He brought Aaron's sons; and Moses put some of the blood on the tip of their right ear, and on the thumb of their right hand, and on the great toe of their right foot; and Moses sprinkled the blood around on the altar.

Lev 8:25 He took the fat, and the fat tail, and all the fat that was on the innards, and the cover of the liver, and the two kidneys, and their fat, and the right thigh;

Lev 8:26 and out of the basket of unleavened bread, that was before YHWH, he took one unleavened cake, and one cake of oiled bread, and one wafer, and placed them on the fat, and on the right thigh.

Lev 8:27 **He put all these in Aaron's hands and in his sons' hands, and waved them for a wave offering before YHWH.**

Lev 8:28 Moses took them from their hands, and burned them on the altar on the burnt offering. They were a consecration for a pleasant aroma. It was an offering made by fire to YHWH.

Lev 8:29 Moses took the breast, and waved it for a wave offering before YHWH. It was Moses' portion of the ram of consecration, as YHWH commanded Moses.

SABBATH Lev 8:30 Moses took some of the anointing oil, and some of the blood which was on the altar, and sprinkled it on Aaron, on his garments, and on his sons, and on his sons' garments with him, and sanctified Aaron, his garments, and his sons, and his sons' garments with him.

page 28

Lev 8:31 Moses said to Aaron and to his sons, "Boil the meat at the door of the Tent of Meeting, and there eat it and the bread that is in the basket of consecration, as I commanded, saying, 'Aaron and his sons shall eat it.'

Lev 8:32 What remains of the meat and of the bread you shall burn with fire.

Lev 8:33 You shall not go out from the door of the Tent of Meeting for seven days, until the days of your consecration are fulfilled: for he shall consecrate you seven days.

Lev 8:34 **What has been done today, so YHWH has commanded to do, to make atonement for you.**

Lev 8:35 You shall stay at the door of the Tent of Meeting day and night seven days, and keep YHWH's command, that you don't die: for so I am commanded."

Lev 8:36 Aaron and his sons did all the things which YHWH commanded by Moses.

MY NOTES

~ EXTRA NOTES ~

CRYPTOGRAM – MALACHI 3:7

A	B	C	D	E	F	G	H	I	J	K	L	M	N	O	P	Q	R	S	T	U	V	W	X	Y	Z
14								3									1	7		20					

```
 _  R  M  _  _  _  A  S  _  _  _  _  U  R  _  A  _  _  R  S
 4  1 19  3 25 15 13 12 14 26  7 19  4 26 19 20  1  4 14 25 13  1  7

 _  U  A  _  _  U  R  _  _  A  S  _  R  M
26 19 20 15 14  2 13 25 20  1 17 13 12 14  7 16 12 13  4  1 19  3

 M  _  S  A  U  S  A  _  _  A
 3 26  7 25 14 25 20 25 13  7 14 17 12 15 14  2 13 17 19 25  9 13 21 25

 _  M  .  R  _  U  R  _  _  M  _  A
25 15 13  3  1 13 25 20  1 17 25 19  3 13  ,  14 17 12 16 22 16 23 23

 R  _  U  R  _  _  _  U  _  S  A  S  _  R
 1 13 25 20  1 17 25 19 26 19 20  7 14 26  7 25 15 13 23 19  1 12

 _  S  _  _  _  _  _  .  U  _  U  S  A
19  4 15 19  7 25  7  6 20 25 26 19 20  7 14 26  15 19 22

 S  _  A  _  _  _  R  _  U  R  ?
 7 15 14 23 23 22 13  1 13 25 20  1 17
```

SCRAMBLE – MATTHEW 5:19

MAURELJES ☐☐☐☐☐☐☐☐☐
                10 12   24 34 17 4 29

TAHZNREA ☐☐☐☐☐☐☐☐
            41 21   36 37 13 6 1

LAELEGI ☐☐☐☐☐☐☐
          43 38 16 40 25 8 23

DOJRAN ☐☐☐☐☐☐
        11 5 32 39 31

SAINI ☐☐☐☐☐
      14 45 33 15 42

BORHEN ☐☐☐☐☐☐
      7 20 18 9 2 22

MACARNEUP ☐☐☐☐☐☐☐☐☐
        27 30   3 19 35 26 44 28

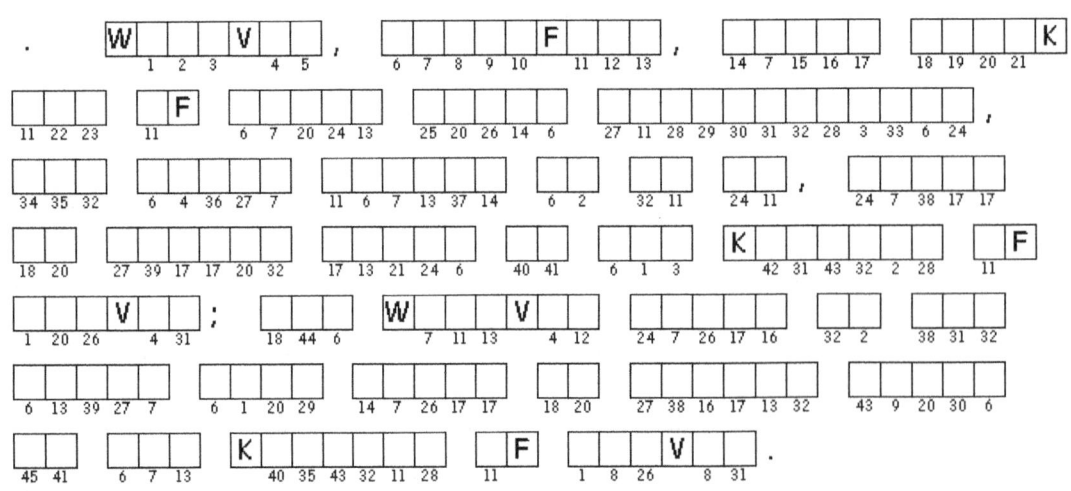

page 30

SHEMINI

שְׁמִינִי

LEVITICUS

It Means: **Eighth**

Our Twenty-Sixth Torah Portion is called Shemini! שְׁמִינִי
Leviticus 9:1 – Leviticus 11:47

PROPHETS: 2 Samuel 6:1-15; Isaiah 65:1-8; 66:15-18; Jeremiah 7:21-8:3; 9:22-24
NEW TESTAMENT: Mark 7:1-23; 9:2-13; Acts 5:1-11; 10-11:18; 15:19-21; 2 Corinthians 6:14-7:1; Galatians 2:11-16; Hebrews 7:1-8:6; 1 Peter 1:14-16

MAKE A MARK

Each time you hear someone say one of the words below make a '/" beside the word. See how many marks you can get!

cloven	
food	
unclean	
body	
evening	
birds	

FIRST FIND

~

If someone mentions a verse or scripture that is NOT in this Torah Portion, see if YOU can be the First to Find it!

SHEMINI

```
I N O I T C N I T S I D I D
F O Y Y E C A E P M N T E A
N O I T A G E R G N O C A N
V T E P S N A E L C N U R I
V B R A T O A Y H B S S T M
K U I H R I I F C A A S H A
A L F O A T V I L D D A E L
V L U O N A M T K A E C N S
E V H F G N N C D N C R F G
S V I A E I E N G U H A T E
S E B A P M V A G O C C K Z
E V A P F O O S L N A E L C
L A F V W B L Y Q M R A M I
C W W U T A C O M M O N R M
```

ABIHU	COMMON	NADAB
ABOMINATION	CONGREGATION	PEACE
ANIMALS	CUD	RAM
BULL	DISTINCTION	SANCTIFY
CALF	EARTHEN	STRANGE
CARCASS	FIRE	UNCLEAN
CLEAN	HOLY	VESSEL
CLOVEN	HOOF	WAVE

Word Search Created by Torah Town

YHWH Accepts Aaron's Offering

<u>SUNDAY</u> Lev 9:1 On the eighth day, Moses called Aaron and his sons, and the elders of Israel;

Lev 9:2 and he said to Aaron, "Take a calf from the herd for a sin offering, and a ram for a burnt offering, without defect, and offer them before YHWH.

Lev 9:3 You shall speak to the children of Israel, saying, 'Take a male goat for a sin offering; and a calf and a lamb, both a year old, without defect, for a burnt offering;

Lev 9:4 and a bull and a ram for peace offerings, to sacrifice before YHWH; and a meal offering mixed with oil: for today YHWH appears to you.'"

Lev 9:5 **They brought what Moses commanded before the Tent of Meeting: and all the congregation came near and stood before YHWH.**

Lev 9:6 Moses said, "This is the thing which YHWH commanded that you should do: and YHWH's glory shall appear to you."

Lev 9:7 Moses said to Aaron, "Draw near to the altar, and offer your sin offering, and your burnt offering, and make atonement for yourself, and for the people; and offer the offering of the people, and make atonement for them; as YHWH commanded."

Lev 9:8 So Aaron came near to the altar, and killed the calf of the sin offering, which was for himself.

Lev 9:9 The sons of Aaron presented the blood to him; and he dipped his finger in the blood, and put it on the horns of the altar, and poured out the blood at the base of the altar:

Lev 9:10 but the fat, and the kidneys, and the cover from the liver of the sin offering, he burned upon the altar; as YHWH commanded Moses.

Lev 9:11 The meat and the skin he burned with fire outside the camp.

Lev 9:12 He killed the burnt offering; and Aaron's sons delivered the blood to him, and he sprinkled it around on the altar.

Lev 9:13 They delivered the burnt offering to him, piece by piece, and the head: and he burned them upon the altar.

Lev 9:14 He washed the innards and the legs, and burned them on the burnt offering on the altar.

Lev 9:15 He presented the people's offering, and took the goat of the sin offering which was for the people, and killed it, and offered it for sin, like the first.

Lev 9:16 He presented the burnt offering, and offered it according to the ordinance.

MONDAY Lev 9:17 He presented the meal offering, and filled his hand from there, and burned it upon the altar, in addition to the burnt offering of the morning.

Lev 9:18 He also killed the bull and the ram, the sacrifice of peace offerings, which was for the people: and Aaron's sons delivered to him the blood, which he sprinkled around on the altar,

Lev 9:19 and the fat of the bull and of the ram, the fat tail, and that which covers the innards, and the kidneys, and the cover of the liver:

Lev 9:20 and they put the fat upon the breasts, and he burned the fat on the altar:

Lev 9:21 and the breasts and the right thigh Aaron waved for a wave offering before YHWH, as Moses commanded.

Lev 9:22 Aaron lifted up his hands toward the people, and blessed them; and he came down from offering the sin offering, and the burnt offering, and the peace offerings.

Lev 9:23 **Moses and Aaron went into the Tent of Meeting, and came out, and blessed the people: and YHWH's glory appeared to all the people.**

TUESDAY Lev 9:24 Fire came out from before YHWH, and consumed the burnt offering and the fat upon the altar. When all the people saw it, they shouted, and fell on their faces.

The Death of Nadab and Abihu

Lev 10:1 Nadab and Abihu, the sons of Aaron, each took his censer, and put fire in it, and laid incense on it, and offered strange fire before YHWH, which he had not commanded them.

Lev 10:2 **Fire came out from before YHWH, and devoured them, and they died before YHWH.**

Lev 10:3 Then Moses said to Aaron, "This is what YHWH spoke of, saying, 'I will show myself holy to those who come near me, and before all the people I will be glorified.'" Aaron held his peace.

Lev 10:4 Moses called Mishael and Elzaphan, the sons of Uzziel the uncle of Aaron, and said to them, "Draw near, carry your brothers from before the sanctuary out of the camp."

Lev 10:5 So they came near, and carried them in their coats out of the camp, as Moses had said.

Lev 10:6 Moses said to Aaron, and to Eleazar and to Ithamar, his sons, "Don't let the hair of your heads go loose, and don't tear your clothes; so that you don't die, and so that he not be angry with all the congregation; but let your brothers, the whole house of Israel, bewail the burning which YHWH has kindled.

Lev 10:7 You shall not go out from the door of the Tent of Meeting, lest you die; for the anointing oil of YHWH is on you." They did according to the word of Moses.

Lev 10:8 Then YHWH said to Aaron,

Lev 10:9 "You and your sons are not to drink wine or strong drink whenever you go into the Tent of Meeting, or you will die. This shall be a statute forever throughout your generations.

Lev 10:10 **You are to make a distinction between the holy and the common, and between the unclean and the clean.**

Lev 10:11 You are to teach the children of Israel all the statutes which YHWH has spoken to them by Moses."

WEDNESDAY Lev 10:12 Moses spoke to Aaron, and to Eleazar and to Ithamar, his sons who were left, *"Take the meal offering that remains of the offerings of YHWH made by fire, and eat it without yeast beside the altar; for it is most holy;*

Lev 10:13 and you shall eat it in a holy place, because it is your portion, and your sons' portion, of the offerings of YHWH made by fire: for so I am commanded.

Lev 10:14 The waved breast and the heaved thigh you shall eat in a clean place, you, and your sons, and your daughters with you: for they are given as your portion, and your sons' portion, out of the sacrifices of the peace offerings of the children of Israel.

Lev 10:15 The heaved thigh and the waved breast they shall bring with the offerings made by fire of the fat, to wave it for a wave offering before YHWH: and it shall be yours, and your sons' with you, as a portion forever; as YHWH has commanded."

THURSDAY Lev 10:16 Moses diligently inquired about the goat of the sin offering, and, behold, it was burned: and he was angry with Eleazar and with Ithamar, the sons of Aaron who were left, saying,

Lev 10:17 "Why haven't you eaten the sin offering in the place of the sanctuary, since it is most holy, and he has given it to you to bear the iniquity of the congregation, to make atonement for them before YHWH?

Lev 10:18 Behold, its blood was not brought into the inner part of the sanctuary: you certainly should have eaten it in the sanctuary, as I commanded."

Lev 10:19 Aaron spoke to Moses, "Behold, today they have offered their sin offering and their burnt offering before YHWH; and such things as these have happened to me. *If I had eaten the sin offering today, would it have been pleasing in YHWH's sight?"*

Lev 10:20 When Moses heard that, it was pleasing in his sight.

Clean and Unclean Animals

FRIDAY Lev 11:1 YHWH spoke to Moses and to Aaron, saying to them,

Lev 11:2 "Speak to the children of Israel, saying, 'These are the living things which you may eat among all the animals that are on the earth.

Lev 11:3 ***Whatever parts the hoof, and is cloven-footed, and chews the cud among the animals, that you may eat.***

Lev 11:4 "'Nevertheless these you shall not eat of those that chew the cud, or of those who part the hoof: the camel, because he chews the cud but doesn't have a parted hoof, he is unclean to you.

Lev 11:5 The cony, because he chews the cud but doesn't have a parted hoof, he is unclean to you.

Lev 11:6 The hare, because she chews the cud but doesn't part the hoof, she is unclean to you.

Lev 11:7 The pig, because he has a split hoof, and is cloven-footed, but doesn't chew the cud, he is unclean to you.

Lev 11:8 Of their meat you shall not eat, and their carcasses you shall not touch; they are unclean to you.

Lev 11:9 "'***These you may eat of all that are in the waters: whatever has fins and scales in the waters, in the seas, and in the rivers, that you may eat.***

Lev 11:10 All that don't have fins and scales in the seas, and in the rivers, of all that move in the waters, and of all the living creatures that are in the waters, they are an abomination to you,

Lev 11:11 and you shall detest them. You shall not eat of their meat, and you shall detest their carcasses.

Lev 11:12 Whatever has no fins nor scales in the waters, that is an abomination to you.

Lev 11:13 "'These you shall detest among the birds; they shall not be eaten, they are an abomination: the eagle, and the vulture, and the black vulture,

Lev 11:14 and the red kite, any kind of black kite,

Lev 11:15 any kind of raven,

MY NOTES

Lev 11:16 the horned owl, the screech owl, and the gull, any kind of hawk,

Lev 11:17 the little owl, the cormorant, the great owl,

Lev 11:18 the white owl, the desert owl, the osprey,

Lev 11:19 the stork, any kind of heron, the hoopoe, and the bat.

Lev 11:20 "'All flying insects that walk on all fours are an abomination to you.

Lev 11:21 **Yet you may eat these: of all winged creeping things that go on all fours, which have legs above their feet, with which to hop on the earth.**

Lev 11:22 Even of these you may eat: any kind of locust, any kind of katydid, any kind of cricket, and any kind of grasshopper.

Lev 11:23 But all winged creeping things which have four feet, are an abomination to you.

Lev 11:24 "'By these you will become unclean: whoever touches their carcass shall be unclean until the evening.

Lev 11:25 Whoever carries any part of their carcass shall wash his clothes, and be unclean until the evening.

Lev 11:26 "'Every animal which parts the hoof, and is not cloven-footed, nor chews the cud, is unclean to you. Everyone who touches them shall be unclean.

Lev 11:27 Whatever goes on its paws, among all animals that go on all fours, they are unclean to you. Whoever touches their carcass shall be unclean until the evening.

Lev 11:28 He who carries their carcass shall wash his clothes, and be unclean until the evening. They are unclean to you.

Lev 11:29 "'These are they which are unclean to you among the creeping things that creep on the earth: the weasel, the rat, any kind of great lizard,

Lev 11:30 the gecko, and the monitor lizard, the wall lizard, the skink, and the chameleon.

Lev 11:31 These are they which are unclean to you among all that creep. Whoever touches them when they are dead, shall be unclean until the evening.

Lev 11:32 On whatever any of them falls when they are dead, it shall be unclean; whether it is any vessel of wood, or clothing, or skin, or sack, whatever vessel it is, with which any work is done, it must be put into water, and it shall be unclean until the evening; then it will be clean.

<u>SABBATH</u> Lev 11:33 Every earthen vessel, into which any of them falls, all that is in it shall be unclean, and you shall break it.

MY NOTES

Lev 11:34 All food which may be eaten, that on which water comes, shall be unclean; and all drink that may be drunk in every such vessel shall be unclean.

Lev 11:35 Everything whereupon part of their carcass falls shall be unclean; whether oven, or range for pots, it shall be broken in pieces: they are unclean, and shall be unclean to you.

Lev 11:36 Nevertheless a spring or a cistern in which water is gathered shall be clean: but that which touches their carcass shall be unclean.

Lev 11:37 If part of their carcass falls on any sowing seed which is to be sown, it is clean.

Lev 11:38 But if water is put on the seed, and part of their carcass falls on it, it is unclean to you.

Lev 11:39 "'If any animal, of which you may eat, dies; he who touches its carcass shall be unclean until the evening.

Lev 11:40 He who eats of its carcass shall wash his clothes, and be unclean until the evening. He also who carries its carcass shall wash his clothes, and be unclean until the evening.

Lev 11:41 **"'Every creeping thing that creeps on the earth is an abomination. It shall not be eaten.**

Lev 11:42 Whatever goes on its belly, and whatever goes on all fours, or whatever has many feet, even all creeping things that creep on the earth, them you shall not eat; for they are an abomination.

Lev 11:43 You shall not make yourselves abominable with any creeping thing that creeps. You shall not make yourselves unclean with them, that you should be defiled thereby.

Lev 11:44 ***For I am YHWH your God. Sanctify yourselves therefore, and be holy; for I am holy. You shall not defile yourselves with any kind of creeping thing that moves on the earth.***

Lev 11:45 For I am YHWH who brought you up out of the land of Egypt, to be your God. You shall therefore be holy, for I am holy.

Lev 11:46 "'This is the law of the animal, and of the bird, and of every living creature that moves in the waters, and of every creature that creeps on the earth,

Lev 11:47 to make a distinction between the unclean and the clean, and between the living thing that may be eaten and the living thing that may not be eaten.'"

VERSE FIND 2 – MARK 9:7

EM,	ING	OUT	A	C	D,	O	H	N	T,	O
BEL		TH	D	S	VO	IS	ON.	SHA		DOW
ME		IM.	ICE	"TH	MY		AN	D	C	STE
OF	D	A	E	C	"	LI	VER	AME		LOU
LOU		TH	IS		CA		OVE			

CROSSWORD – ISAIAH 65:1-13

Across
8. _____ in gardens
10. a person who serves
13. to be let down
14. who eat _____ flesh
15. yes, I will _____ into their bosom
17. a people who _____ me to my face continually
19. I am _____ of by those who didn't ask.
20. I am _____ by those who didn't seek me.

Down
1. I have spread out my hands all day to a _____ people
2. and broth of _____ things is in their vessels
3. to desire food to eat
4. and _____ me on the hills
5. a bunch of cattle
6. another word for children
7. and _____ incense on bricks
8. a weapon larger than a knife
9. to hear with interest
11. parched for something to drink
12. to kill mercilessly
16. a very large hill
18. the opposite of good

TAZRIA

תַזְרִיעַ

LEVITICUS

It Means: **She Bears Seed**

Our Twenty-Seventh Torah Portion is called Tazria! תַזְרִיעַ
Leviticus 12:1 – Leviticus 13:59
PROPHETS: 2 Kings 4:42-5:19
NEW TESTAMENT: Mark 1:40-45; 5:1-43; Luke 2:22-24; 5:12-16; 7:18-23; Romans 6

MAKE A MARK

Each time you hear someone say one of the words below make a '/" beside the word. See how many marks you can get!

itch	
scab	
tattoo	
bald	
mold	
mildew	

FIRST FIND

~

If someone mentions a verse or scripture that is NOT in this Torah Portion, see if YOU can be the First to Find it!

TAZRIA

```
Q G I T C H I N G J N J P T
V H P R O N O U N C E U E N
H B L E M I S H J X R M E E
T S D L A B N E N I L C V M
R L P L A G U E F V N I M R
I M I C H W X I G A T I N A
B H S O O I C U R C L Q I G
D S O O B A Y A U D N I K M
L E L Q T S E R E D D I S H
I L R I O P T W C S H A V E
H F O R P S H A I R N E Z Z
C N P A E E Z E N I M A X E
Y E O D G R E E N I S H A Y
L Z F E S I C M U C R I C C
```

APPEARANCE	FLESH	PLAGUE
BALD	GARMENT	PRONOUNCE
BLEMISH	GREENISH	PURIFICATION
BOIL	HAIR	REDDISH
CHILDBIRTH	ITCHING	SCAB
CIRCUMCISE	LEPROSY	SHAVE
DESTRUCTIVE	LINEN	SKIN
EXAMINE	MILDEW	WOOL

Word Search Created by Torah Town

LEVITICUS 16:12-13

He shall take a censer full of coals of fire from off the altar before Yahweh, and two handfuls of sweet incense beaten small, and bring it within the veil: and he shall put the incense on the fire before Yahweh, that the cloud of the incense may cover the mercy seat that is on the testimony, so that he will not die.

Purification After Childbirth

<u>SUNDAY</u> Lev 12:1 YHWH spoke to Moses, saying,

Lev 12:2 "Speak to the children of Israel, saying, 'If a woman conceives, and bears a male child, then she shall be unclean seven days; as in the days of her monthly period she shall be unclean.

Lev 12:3 ***In the eighth day the flesh of his foreskin shall be circumcised.***

Lev 12:4 She shall continue in the blood of purification thirty-three days. She shall not touch any holy thing, nor come into the sanctuary, until the days of her purifying are completed.

Lev 12:5 But if she bears a female child, then she shall be unclean two weeks, as in her period; and she shall continue in the blood of purification sixty-six days.

Lev 12:6 "'When the days of her purification are completed, for a son, or for a daughter, she shall bring to the priest at the door of the Tent of Meeting, a year old lamb for a burnt offering, and a young pigeon, or a turtledove, for a sin offering:

Lev 12:7 and he shall offer it before YHWH, and make atonement for her; and she shall be cleansed from the fountain of her blood. "'This is the law for her who bears, whether a male or a female.

Lev 12:8 If she cannot afford a lamb, then she shall take two turtledoves, or two young pigeons; the one for a burnt offering, and the other for a sin offering: and the priest shall make atonement for her, and she shall be clean.'"

Laws About Leprosy

Lev 13:1 YHWH spoke to Moses and to Aaron, saying,

Lev 13:2 "When a man shall have a rising in his body's skin, or a scab, or a bright spot, and it becomes in the skin of his body the plague of leprosy, then he shall be brought to Aaron the priest, or to one of his sons, the priests:

Lev 13:3 and the priest shall examine the plague in the skin of the body: and if the hair in the plague has turned white, and the appearance of the plague is deeper than the body's skin, it is the plague of leprosy; and the priest shall examine him, and pronounce him unclean.

Lev 13:4 If the bright spot is white in the skin of his body, and its appearance isn't deeper than the skin, and its hair hasn't turned white, then the priest shall isolate the infected person for seven days.

Lev 13:5 The priest shall examine him on the seventh day, and, behold, if in his eyes the plague is arrested, and the plague hasn't spread in the skin, then the priest shall isolate him for seven more days.

MONDAY Lev 13:6 The priest shall examine him again on the seventh day; and behold, if the plague has faded, and the plague hasn't spread in the skin, then the priest shall pronounce him clean. It is a scab. He shall wash his clothes, and be clean.

Lev 13:7 But if the scab spreads on the skin, after he has shown himself to the priest for his cleansing, he shall show himself to the priest again.

Lev 13:8 The priest shall examine him; and behold, if the scab has spread on the skin, then the priest shall pronounce him unclean. It is leprosy.

Lev 13:9 *"When the plague of leprosy is in a man, then he shall be brought to the priest;*

Lev 13:10 and the priest shall examine him. Behold, if there is a white rising in the skin, and it has turned the hair white, and there is raw flesh in the rising,

Lev 13:11 it is a chronic leprosy in the skin of his body, and the priest shall pronounce him unclean. He shall not isolate him, for he is already unclean.

Lev 13:12 "If the leprosy breaks out all over the skin, and the leprosy covers all the skin of the infected person from his head even to his feet, as far as it appears to the priest;

Lev 13:13 then the priest shall examine him; and, behold, if the leprosy has covered all his flesh, he shall pronounce him clean of the plague. It has all turned white: he is clean.

Lev 13:14 But whenever raw flesh appears in him, he shall be unclean.

Lev 13:15 The priest shall examine the raw flesh, and pronounce him unclean: the raw flesh is unclean. It is leprosy.

Lev 13:16 Or if the raw flesh turns again, and is changed to white, then he shall come to the priest;

Lev 13:17 and the priest shall examine him; and, behold, if the plague has turned white, then the priest shall pronounce him clean of the plague. He is clean.

TUESDAY Lev 13:18 "When the body has a boil on its skin, and it has healed,

Lev 13:19 and in the place of the boil there is a white rising, or a bright spot, reddish-white, then it shall be shown to the priest;

MY NOTES

Lev 13:20 and the priest shall examine it; and behold, if its appearance is lower than the skin, and its hair has turned white, then the priest shall pronounce him unclean. It is the plague of leprosy. It has broken out in the boil.

Lev 13:21 But if the priest examines it, and behold, there are no white hairs in it, and it isn't deeper than the skin, but is dim, then the priest shall isolate him seven days.

Lev 13:22 **If it spreads in the skin, then the priest shall pronounce him unclean. It is a plague.**

Lev 13:23 But if the bright spot stays in its place, and hasn't spread, it is the scar from the boil; and the priest shall pronounce him clean.

WEDNESDAY Lev 13:24 "Or when the body has a burn from fire on its skin, and the raw flesh of the burn becomes a bright spot, reddish-white, or white,

Lev 13:25 then the priest shall examine it; and behold, if the hair in the bright spot has turned white, and its appearance is deeper than the skin; it is leprosy. It has broken out in the burning, and the priest shall pronounce him unclean. It is the plague of leprosy.

Lev 13:26 But if the priest examines it, and behold, there is no white hair in the bright spot, and it isn't lower than the skin, but is faded; then the priest shall isolate him seven days.

Lev 13:27 The priest shall examine him on the seventh day. If it has spread in the skin, then the priest shall pronounce him unclean. **It is the plague of leprosy.**

Lev 13:28 If the bright spot stays in its place, and hasn't spread in the skin, but is faded, it is the swelling from the burn, and the priest shall pronounce him clean; for it is the scar from the burn.

THURSDAY Lev 13:29 "When a man or woman has a plague on the head or on the beard,

Lev 13:30 then the priest shall examine the plague; and behold, if its appearance is deeper than the skin, and the hair in it is yellow and thin, then the priest shall pronounce him unclean: it is an itch, it is leprosy of the head or of the beard.

Lev 13:31 If the priest examines the plague of itching, and behold, its appearance isn't deeper than the skin, and there is no black hair in it, then the priest shall isolate the person infected with itching seven days.

Lev 13:32 On the seventh day the priest shall examine the plague; and behold, if the itch hasn't spread, and there is no yellow hair in it, and the appearance of the itch isn't deeper than the skin,

MY NOTES

Lev 13:33 then he shall be shaved, but he shall not shave the itch; and the priest shall shut him up who has the itch seven more days.

Lev 13:34 On the seventh day, the priest shall examine the itch; and behold, if the itch hasn't spread in the skin, and its appearance isn't deeper than the skin, then the priest shall pronounce him clean. He shall wash his clothes, and be clean.

Lev 13:35 But if the itch spreads in the skin after his cleansing,

Lev 13:36 then the priest shall examine him; and behold, if the itch has spread in the skin, the priest shall not look for the yellow hair; he is unclean.

Lev 13:37 **But if in his eyes the itch is arrested, and black hair has grown in it; the itch is healed, he is clean. The priest shall pronounce him clean.**

Lev 13:38 "When a man or a woman has bright spots in the skin of the body, even white bright spots;

Lev 13:39 then the priest shall examine them; and behold, if the bright spots on the skin of their body are a dull white, it is a harmless rash, it has broken out in the skin; he is clean.

<u>FRIDAY</u> Lev 13:40 **"If a man's hair has fallen from his head, he is bald. He is clean.**

Lev 13:41 If his hair has fallen off from the front part of his head, he is forehead bald. He is clean.

Lev 13:42 But if there is in the bald head, or the bald forehead, a reddish-white plague; it is leprosy breaking out in his bald head, or his bald forehead.

Lev 13:43 Then the priest shall examine him; and, behold, if the rising of the plague is reddish-white in his bald head, or in his bald forehead, like the appearance of leprosy in the skin of the flesh,

Lev 13:44 he is a leprous man. He is unclean. The priest shall surely pronounce him unclean. His plague is on his head.

Lev 13:45 "The leper in whom the plague is shall wear torn clothes, and the hair of his head shall hang loose. He shall cover his upper lip, and shall cry, 'Unclean! Unclean!'

Lev 13:46 All the days in which the plague is in him he shall be unclean. He is unclean. He shall dwell alone. Outside of the camp shall be his dwelling.

Lev 13:47 "The garment also that the plague of leprosy is in, whether it is a woolen garment, or a linen garment;

Lev 13:48 whether it is in warp, or woof; of linen, or of wool; whether in a skin, or in anything made of skin;

Lev 13:49 if the plague is greenish or reddish in the garment, or in the skin, or in the warp, or in the woof, or in anything made of skin; it is the plague of leprosy, and shall be shown to the priest.

Lev 13:50 **The priest shall examine the plague, and isolate the plague seven days.**

Lev 13:51 He shall examine the plague on the seventh day. If the plague has spread in the garment, either in the warp, or in the woof, or in the skin, whatever use the skin is used for, the plague is a destructive mildew. It is unclean.

Lev 13:52 He shall burn the garment, whether the warp or the woof, in wool or in linen, or anything of skin, in which the plague is: for it is a destructive mildew. It shall be burned in the fire.

Lev 13:53 "If the priest examines it, and behold, the plague hasn't spread in the garment, either in the warp, or in the woof, or in anything of skin;

Lev 13:54 then the priest shall command that they wash the thing in which the plague is, and he shall isolate it seven more days.

SABBATH Lev 13:55 Then the priest shall examine it, after the plague is washed; and behold, if the plague hasn't changed its color, and the plague hasn't spread, it is unclean; you shall burn it in the fire. *It is a mildewed spot, whether the bareness is inside or outside.*

Lev 13:56 If the priest looks, and behold, the plague has faded after it is washed, then he shall tear it out of the garment, or out of the skin, or out of the warp, or out of the woof:

Lev 13:57 and if it appears again in the garment, either in the warp, or in the woof, or in anything of skin, it is spreading. You shall burn with fire that in which the plague is.

Lev 13:58 The garment, either the warp, or the woof, or whatever thing of skin it is, which you shall wash, if the plague has departed from them, then it shall be washed the second time, and it will be clean."

Lev 13:59 *This is the law of the plague of mildew in a garment of wool or linen, either in the warp, or the woof, or in anything of skin, to pronounce it clean, or to pronounce it unclean.*

VERSE FIND – LUKE 2:22

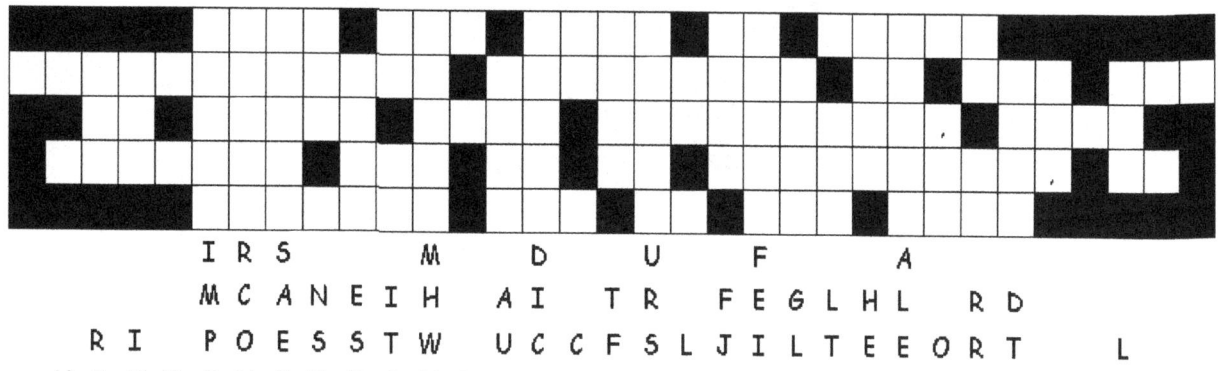

HIDDEN VERSE – ROMANS 6:16

```
D O N T Y G O U K N O W G T H
A T W H I E N Y O U P T N R E
S E N V T Y T O U T R C I S E
L V I E S N A S H S E E V E R
V N A N E T S O G A C P O N D
G O B I E Y U N S O N S L M E
O N T E Y G I O U A E E R E T
H A E S H R E S R S R R V A N
P T S T A O F S W U E H O M E
V R F C E R Y E O O V U O B E
Y U E W H H O N O R E E T H E
L R O Y F S I D N E R T O D E
A T H O A R O N F N L O Y A L
O B E D I R E I N E C E T O R
I G H T E O P K U G S N E S S
```

CARING
GENEROUS
GIVING
HONOR
KINDNESS
LOVING
LOYAL
PATIENT
PRAYER
RESPECT
REVERENCE
THOUGHTFUL

___'_ ___ ____ ____ ____ ___

_____ _____ ___ _____

___ ___ _____, ___ ___

____ _____ __ _____ ___

____; _____ __ ___ __ _____,

__ __ _____ __ _____?

page 51

METZORA

מְצֹרָע

LEVITICUS

It Means: **Infected One**

Our Twenty-Eighth Torah Portion is called Metzora! מְצֹרָע

Leviticus 14:1 – Leviticus 15:33

PROPHETS: 2 Kings 7:3-20
NEW TESTAMENT: Matthew 8:1-17; 9:18-26; Luke 10:1-42; 17:1-37; Romans 6:15-23; Hebrews 13:4

MAKE A MARK

Each time you hear someone say one of the words below make a '✓" beside the word. See how many marks you can get!

toe	
ear	
water	
clean	
leprosy	
house	

FIRST FIND

~

If someone mentions a verse or scripture that is NOT in this Torah Portion, see if YOU can be the First to Find it!

METZORA

```
T S H T N E V E S A H Y S C
U F Q P I D G E O N R D P T
R P E N A A N A C T A I R E
T N O I S S E S S O P S I K
L K L S I H O G Y V A C N T
E C H F S P O R D T D H K H
D W C T E Y A U O Q E A L U
O F A H H U H N S V F R E M
V W T T T G E E J E I G C B
E A O C E M I B T S L E E E
B O N R E R M E D S E U A O
F A O N S C A R L E T C R T
S O T R A D E C X L A A L O
P A U N C L E A N N E S S A
```

ATONEMENT	FOOT	SEVENTH
BATHE	HOUSE	SPRINKLE
CANAAN	HYSSOP	THUMB
CEDAR	PIDGEON	TOE
DEFILE	POOR	TURTLEDOVE
DISCHARGE	POSSESSION	UNCLEANNESS
EAR	SANCTUARY	VESSEL
EIGHTH	SCARLET	WATER

Word Search Created by Torah Town

Leviticus 14:53

but he shall let the living bird go out of the city into the open field. So shall he make atonement for the house; and it shall be clean."

Laws for Cleansing Lepers

SUNDAY Lev 14:1 YHWH spoke to Moses, saying,

Lev 14:2 "This shall be the law of the leper in the day of his cleansing. He shall be brought to the priest,

Lev 14:3 and the priest shall go out of the camp. The priest shall examine him, and behold, if the plague of leprosy is healed in the leper,

Lev 14:4 then the priest shall command them to take for him who is to be cleansed two living clean birds, and cedar wood, and scarlet, and hyssop.

Lev 14:5 ***The priest shall command them to kill one of the birds in an earthen vessel over running water.***

Lev 14:6 As for the living bird, he shall take it, and the cedar wood, and the scarlet, and the hyssop, and shall dip them and the living bird in the blood of the bird that was killed over the running water.

Lev 14:7 He shall sprinkle on him who is to be cleansed from the leprosy seven times, and shall pronounce him clean, and shall let the living bird go into the open field.

Lev 14:8 "He who is to be cleansed shall wash his clothes, and shave off all his hair, and bathe himself in water; and he shall be clean. After that he shall come into the camp, but shall dwell outside his tent seven days.

Lev 14:9 It shall be on the seventh day, that he shall shave all his hair off his head and his beard and his eyebrows, even all his hair he shall shave off. He shall wash his clothes, and he shall bathe his body in water, then he shall be clean.

Lev 14:10 "On the eighth day he shall take two male lambs without defect, and one ewe lamb a year old without defect, and three tenths of an ephah of fine flour for a meal offering, mingled with oil, and one log of oil.

Lev 14:11 The priest who cleanses him shall set the man who is to be cleansed, and those things, before YHWH, at the door of the Tent of Meeting.

Lev 14:12 "The priest shall take one of the male lambs, and offer him for a trespass offering, with the log of oil, and wave them for a wave offering before YHWH.

MONDAY Lev 14:13 He shall kill the male lamb in the place where they kill the sin offering and the burnt offering, in the place of the sanctuary; for as the sin offering is the priest's, so is the trespass offering. It is most holy.

Lev 14:14 The priest shall take some of the blood of the trespass offering, and the priest shall put it on the tip of the right ear of him who is to be cleansed, and on the thumb of his right hand, and on the big toe of his right foot.

Lev 14:15 **The priest shall take some of the log of oil, and pour it into the palm of his own left hand.**

Lev 14:16 The priest shall dip his right finger in the oil that is in his left hand, and shall sprinkle some of the oil with his finger seven times before YHWH.

Lev 14:17 The priest shall put some of the rest of the oil that is in his hand on the tip of the right ear of him who is to be cleansed, and on the thumb of his right hand, and on the big toe of his right foot, upon the blood of the trespass offering.

Lev 14:18 The rest of the oil that is in the priest's hand he shall put on the head of him who is to be cleansed, and the priest shall make atonement for him before YHWH.

Lev 14:19 "The priest shall offer the sin offering, and make atonement for him who is to be cleansed because of his uncleanness: and afterward he shall kill the burnt offering;

Lev 14:20 and the priest shall offer the burnt offering and the meal offering on the altar. The priest shall make atonement for him, and he shall be clean.

TUESDAY Lev 14:21 "If he is poor, and can't afford so much, then he shall take one male lamb for a trespass offering to be waved, to make atonement for him, and one tenth of an ephah of fine flour mingled with oil for a meal offering, and a log of oil;

Lev 14:22 and two turtledoves, or two young pigeons, such as he is able to afford; and the one shall be a sin offering, and the other a burnt offering.

Lev 14:23 **"On the eighth day he shall bring them for his cleansing to the priest, to the door of the Tent of Meeting, before YHWH.**

Lev 14:24 The priest shall take the lamb of the trespass offering, and the log of oil, and the priest shall wave them for a wave offering before YHWH.

Lev 14:25 He shall kill the lamb of the trespass offering. The priest shall take some of the blood of the trespass offering and put it on the tip of the right ear of him who is to be cleansed, and on the thumb of his right hand, and on the big toe of his right foot.

Lev 14:26 The priest shall pour some of the oil into the palm of his own left hand;

MY NOTES

Lev 14:27 and the priest shall sprinkle with his right finger some of the oil that is in his left hand seven times before YHWH.

Lev 14:28 Then the priest shall put some of the oil that is in his hand on the tip of the right ear of him who is to be cleansed, and on the thumb of his right hand, and on the big toe of his right foot, on the place of the blood of the trespass offering.

Lev 14:29 The rest of the oil that is in the priest's hand he shall put on the head of him who is to be cleansed, to make atonement for him before YHWH.

Lev 14:30 He shall offer one of the turtledoves, or of the young pigeons, such as he is able to afford,

Lev 14:31 even such as he is able to afford, the one for a sin offering, and the other for a burnt offering, with the meal offering. The priest shall make atonement for him who is to be cleansed before YHWH."

Lev 14:32 This is the law for him in whom is the plague of leprosy, who is not able to afford the sacrifice for his cleansing.

Laws for Cleansing Houses

WEDNESDAY Lev 14:33 YHWH spoke to Moses and to Aaron, saying,

Lev 14:34 "When you have come into the land of Canaan, which I give to you for a possession, and I put a spreading mildew in a house in the land of your possession,

Lev 14:35 then he who owns the house shall come and tell the priest, saying, 'There seems to me to be some sort of plague in the house.'

Lev 14:36 The priest shall command that they empty the house, before the priest goes in to examine the plague, that all that is in the house not be made unclean. Afterward the priest shall go in to inspect the house.

Lev 14:37 He shall examine the plague; and behold, if the plague is in the walls of the house with hollow streaks, greenish or reddish, and it appears to be deeper than the wall;

Lev 14:38 then the priest shall go out of the house to the door of the house, and shut up the house seven days.

Lev 14:39 The priest shall come again on the seventh day, and look. If the plague has spread in the walls of the house,

Lev 14:40 then the priest shall command that they take out the stones in which is the plague, and cast them into an unclean place outside of the city:

Lev 14:41 and he shall cause the inside of the house to be scraped all over, and they shall pour out the mortar, that they scraped off, outside of the city into an unclean place.

Lev 14:42 They shall take other stones, and put them in the place of those stones; and he shall take other mortar, and shall plaster the house.

Lev 14:43 "If the plague comes again, and breaks out in the house, after he has taken out the stones, and after he has scraped the house, and after it was plastered;

Lev 14:44 **then the priest shall come in and look; and behold, if the plague has spread in the house, it is a destructive mildew in the house. It is unclean.**

Lev 14:45 He shall break down the house, its stones, and its timber, and all the house's mortar. He shall carry them out of the city into an unclean place.

Lev 14:46 "Moreover he who goes into the house while it is shut up shall be unclean until the evening.

Lev 14:47 He who lies down in the house shall wash his clothes; and he who eats in the house shall wash his clothes.

Lev 14:48 "If the priest shall come in, and examine it, and behold, the plague hasn't spread in the house, after the house was plastered, then the priest shall pronounce the house clean, because the plague is healed.

Lev 14:49 To cleanse the house he shall take two birds, and cedar wood, and scarlet, and hyssop.

Lev 14:50 He shall kill one of the birds in an earthen vessel over running water.

Lev 14:51 He shall take the cedar wood, and the hyssop, and the scarlet, and the living bird, and dip them in the blood of the slain bird, and in the running water, and sprinkle the house seven times.

Lev 14:52 He shall cleanse the house with the blood of the bird, and with the running water, with the living bird, with the cedar wood, with the hyssop, and with the scarlet;

Lev 14:53 but he shall let the living bird go out of the city into the open field. So shall he make atonement for the house; and it shall be clean."

THURSDAY Lev 14:54 This is the law for any plague of leprosy, and for an itch,

Lev 14:55 and for the destructive mildew of a garment, and for a house,

Lev 14:56 and for a rising, and for a scab, and for a bright spot;

Lev 14:57 **to teach when it is unclean, and when it is clean. This is the law of leprosy.**

Laws About Bodily Discharges

Lev 15:1 YHWH spoke to Moses and to Aaron, saying,

Lev 15:2 "Speak to the children of Israel, and tell them, 'When any man has a discharge from his body, because of his discharge he is unclean.

Lev 15:3 This shall be his uncleanness in his discharge: whether his body runs with his discharge, or his body has stopped from his discharge, it is his uncleanness.

Lev 15:4 "'Every bed whereon he who has the discharge lies shall be unclean; and everything he sits on shall be unclean.

Lev 15:5 Whoever touches his bed shall wash his clothes, and bathe himself in water, and be unclean until the evening.

Lev 15:6 He who sits on anything whereon the man who has the discharge sat shall wash his clothes, and bathe himself in water, and be unclean until the evening.

Lev 15:7 "'He who touches the body of him who has the discharge shall wash his clothes, and bathe himself in water, and be unclean until the evening.

Lev 15:8 "'If he who has the discharge spits on him who is clean, then he shall wash his clothes, and bathe himself in water, and be unclean until the evening.

Lev 15:9 **"'Whatever saddle he who has the discharge rides on shall be unclean.**

Lev 15:10 Whoever touches anything that was under him shall be unclean until the evening. He who carries those things shall wash his clothes, and bathe himself in water, and be unclean until the evening.

Lev 15:11 "'Whoever he who has the discharge touches, without having rinsed his hands in water, he shall wash his clothes, and bathe himself in water, and be unclean until the evening.

Lev 15:12 "'The earthen vessel, which he who has the discharge touches, shall be broken; and every vessel of wood shall be rinsed in water.

Lev 15:13 "'When he who has a discharge is cleansed of his discharge, then he shall count to himself seven days for his cleansing, and wash his clothes; and he shall bathe his flesh in running water, and shall be clean.

Lev 15:14 "'On the eighth day he shall take two turtledoves, or two young pigeons, and come before YHWH to the door of the Tent of Meeting, and give them to the priest:

MY NOTES

Lev 15:15 and the priest shall offer them, the one for a sin offering, and the other for a burnt offering. The priest shall make atonement for him before YHWH for his discharge.

FRIDAY Lev 15:16 "'If any man has an emission of semen, then he shall bathe all his flesh in water, and be unclean until the evening.

Lev 15:17 Every garment, and every skin, whereon the semen is, shall be washed with water, and be unclean until the evening.

Lev 15:18 If a man lies with a woman and there is an emission of semen, they shall both bathe themselves in water, and be unclean until the evening.

Lev 15:19 "'If a woman has a discharge, and her discharge in her flesh is blood, she shall be in her impurity seven days: and whoever touches her shall be unclean until the evening.

Lev 15:20 "'Everything that she lies on in her impurity shall be unclean. Everything also that she sits on shall be unclean.

Lev 15:21 Whoever touches her bed shall wash his clothes, and bathe himself in water, and be unclean until the evening.

Lev 15:22 Whoever touches anything that she sits on shall wash his clothes, and bathe himself in water, and be unclean until the evening.

Lev 15:23 If it is on the bed, or on anything whereon she sits, when he touches it, he shall be unclean until the evening.

Lev 15:24 "'If any man lies with her, and her monthly flow is on him, he shall be unclean seven days; and every bed whereon he lies shall be unclean.

Lev 15:25 "'If a woman has a discharge of her blood many days not in the time of her period, or if she has a discharge beyond the time of her period; all the days of the discharge of her uncleanness shall be as in the days of her period: she is unclean.

Lev 15:26 Every bed whereon she lies all the days of her discharge shall be to her as the bed of her period: and everything whereon she sits shall be unclean, as the uncleanness of her period.

Lev 15:27 Whoever touches these things shall be unclean, and shall wash his clothes, and bathe himself in water, and be unclean until the evening.

Lev 15:28 **"'But if she is cleansed of her discharge, then she shall count to herself seven days, and after that she shall be clean.**

MY NOTES

SABBATH Lev 15:29 On the eighth day she shall take two turtledoves, or two young pigeons, and bring them to the priest, to the door of the Tent of Meeting.

Lev 15:30 The priest shall offer the one for a sin offering, and the other for a burnt offering; and the priest shall make atonement for her before YHWH for the uncleanness of her discharge.

Lev 15:31 "***Thus you shall separate the children of Israel from their uncleanness, so they will not die in their uncleanness, when they defile my tabernacle that is among them.***'"

Lev 15:32 This is the law of him who has a discharge, and of him who has an emission of semen, so that he is unclean thereby;

Lev 15:33 and of her who has her period, and of a man or woman who has a discharge, and of him who lies with her who is unclean.

MY NOTES

~ EXTRA NOTES ~

VERSE FIND – HEBREWS 13:4

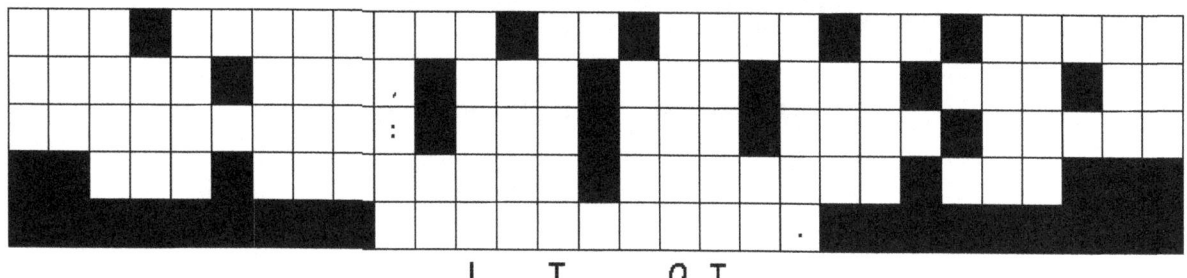

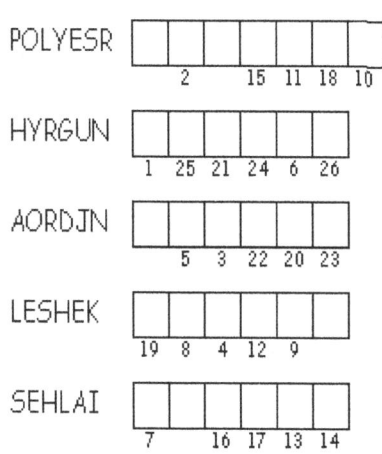

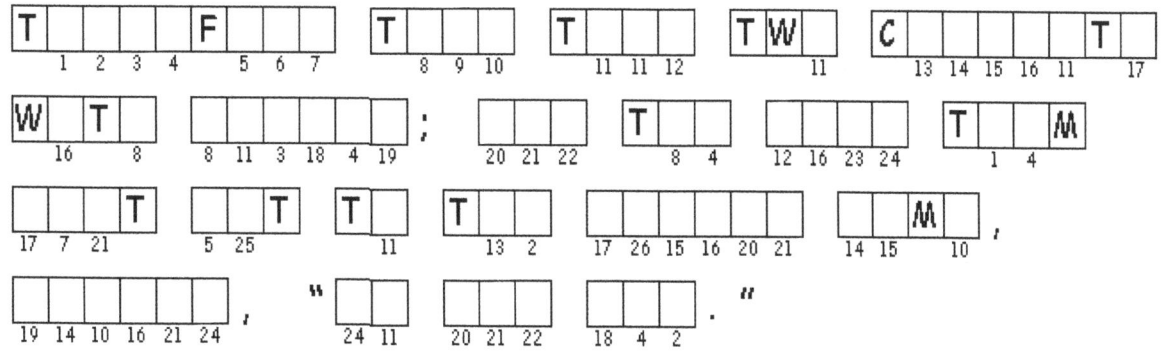

SCRAMBLE – 2 KINGS 7:14

ACHAREI MOT
אַחֲרֵי מוֹת
LEVITICUS

It Means: **After The Death**

Our Twenty-ninth Torah Portion is called Acharei Mot!

אַחֲרֵי מוֹת

Leviticus 16:1 – Leviticus 18:30

PROPHETS: Malachi 3 - 4
NEW TESTAMENT: John 7:1-10:21; Romans 3:19-28; 9:30-10:13; 1 Corinthians 5:1-13; 2 Corinthians 2:1-17; Galatians 3:10-14; Hebrews 7:23-10:25

MAKE A MARK

Each time you hear someone say one of the words below make a '/" beside the word. See how many marks you can get!

goat	
sheep	
family	
laws	
Yeshua	
God	

FIRST FIND

~

If someone mentions a verse or scripture that is NOT in this Torah Portion, see if YOU can be the First to Find it!

ACHAREI MOT

```
F X S E V I T A L E R X T O D
T N S H O U S E H O L D L G L
P O P C H R E V O C N U E V E
Y I W J A Y L L K H W N S S I
G S S E X P L A T W E D E E F
E S E E T E E A N R O E I H C
S E C S W N B G A D I T T A O
S R N D E B E T O N T I I D N
E G A R A T I M C A S M U E F
N S N S E O U E E M T O Q L E
D N I N N S N T O N V V I I S
E A D S W S N T A E O V N F S
K R R M E K S E I T U T I E T
A T O M G U C L C I S Z A D I
N O Q S C R E N G I E R O F D
```

ATONEMENT	FOREIGNER	RELATIVES
CENSER	GENERATIONS	SABBATH
CONFESS	HOUSEHOLD	SCAPEGOAT
CUSTOMS	INCENSE	STATUTES
DEFILED	INIQUITIES	TRANSGRESSION
DWELL	LAND	UNCOVER
EGYPT	NAKEDNESS	VEIL
FIELD	ORDINANCES	VOMITED

Word Search Created by Torah Town

ROSH HASHANA
FEAST OF TRUMPETS

The Day of Atonement

SUNDAY Lev 16:1 YHWH spoke to Moses, after the death of the two sons of Aaron, when they came near before YHWH, and died;

Lev 16:2 and YHWH said to Moses, "Tell Aaron your brother, not to come at all times into the Most Holy Place within the veil, before the mercy seat which is on the ark; lest he die: for I will appear in the cloud on the mercy seat.

Lev 16:3 "Aaron shall come into the sanctuary with a young bull for a sin offering, and a ram for a burnt offering.

Lev 16:4 He shall put on the holy linen coat. He shall have the linen breeches on his body, and shall put on the linen sash, and he shall be clothed with the linen turban. They are the holy garments. He shall bathe his body in water, and put them on.

Lev 16:5 He shall take from the congregation of the children of Israel two male goats for a sin offering, and one ram for a burnt offering.

Lev 16:6 "Aaron shall offer the bull of the sin offering, which is for himself, and make atonement for himself and for his house.

Lev 16:7 He shall take the two goats, and set them before YHWH at the door of the Tent of Meeting.

Lev 16:8 **Aaron shall cast lots for the two goats; one lot for YHWH, and the other lot for the scapegoat.**

Lev 16:9 Aaron shall present the goat on which the lot fell for YHWH, and offer him for a sin offering.

Lev 16:10 But the goat on which the lot fell for the scapegoat shall be presented alive before YHWH, to make atonement for him, to send him away as the scapegoat into the wilderness.

Lev 16:11 "Aaron shall present the bull of the sin offering, which is for himself, and shall make atonement for himself and for his house, and shall kill the bull of the sin offering which is for himself.

Lev 16:12 He shall take a censer full of coals of fire from off the altar before YHWH, and two handfuls of sweet incense beaten small, and bring it within the veil:

Lev 16:13 and he shall put the incense on the fire before YHWH, that the cloud of the incense may cover the mercy seat that is on the testimony, so that he will not die.

Lev 16:14 He shall take some of the blood of the bull, and sprinkle it with his finger on the mercy seat on the east; and before the mercy seat he shall sprinkle some of the blood with his finger seven times.

Lev 16:15 "Then he shall kill the goat of the sin offering, that is for the people, and bring his blood within the veil, and do with his blood as he did with the blood of the bull, and sprinkle it on the mercy seat, and before the mercy seat.

Lev 16:16 He shall make atonement for the Holy Place, because of the uncleanness of the children of Israel, and because of their transgressions, even all their sins; and so he shall do for the Tent of Meeting, that dwells with them in the middle of their uncleanness.

Lev 16:17 No one shall be in the Tent of Meeting when he enters to make atonement in the Holy Place, until he comes out, and has made atonement for himself and for his household, and for all the assembly of Israel.

MONDAY Lev 16:18 "He shall go out to the altar that is before YHWH and make atonement for it, and shall take some of the bull's blood, and some of the goat's blood, and put it around on the horns of the altar.

Lev 16:19 He shall sprinkle some of the blood on it with his finger seven times, and cleanse it, and make it holy from the uncleanness of the children of Israel.

Lev 16:20 "When he has finished atoning for the Holy Place, the Tent of Meeting, and the altar, he shall present the live goat.

Lev 16:21 Aaron shall lay both his hands on the head of the live goat, and confess over him all the iniquities of the children of Israel, and all their transgressions, even all their sins; and he shall put them on the head of the goat, and shall send him away into the wilderness by the hand of a man who is in readiness.

Lev 16:22 *The goat shall carry all their iniquities on himself to a solitary land, and he shall release the goat in the wilderness.*

Lev 16:23 "Aaron shall come into the Tent of Meeting, and shall take off the linen garments, which he put on when he went into the Holy Place, and shall leave them there.

Lev 16:24 Then he shall bathe himself in water in a holy place, and put on his garments, and come out and offer his burnt offering and the burnt offering of the people, and make atonement for himself and for the people.

TUESDAY Lev 16:25 The fat of the sin offering he shall burn on the altar.

Lev 16:26 *"He who lets the goat go as the scapegoat shall wash his clothes, and bathe his flesh in water, and afterward he shall come into the camp.*

Lev 16:27 The bull for the sin offering, and the goat for the sin offering, whose blood was brought in to make atonement in the Holy Place, shall be carried outside the camp; and they shall burn their skins, their flesh, and their dung with fire.

Lev 16:28 He who burns them shall wash his clothes, and bathe his flesh in water, and afterward he shall come into the camp.

Lev 16:29 "It shall be a statute to you forever: in the seventh month, on the tenth day of the month, you shall afflict your souls, and shall do no kind of work, the native-born, or the stranger who lives as a foreigner among you:

Lev 16:30 for on this day shall atonement be made for you, to cleanse you; from all your sins you shall be clean before YHWH.

Lev 16:31 **It is a Sabbath of solemn rest to you, and you shall afflict your souls. It is a statute forever.**

Lev 16:32 The priest, who is anointed and who is consecrated to be priest in his father's place, shall make the atonement, and shall put on the linen garments, even the holy garments.

Lev 16:33 Then he shall make atonement for the Holy Sanctuary; and he shall make atonement for the Tent of Meeting and for the altar; and he shall make atonement for the priests and for all the people of the assembly.

Lev 16:34 "This shall be an everlasting statute for you, to make atonement for the children of Israel once in the year because of all their sins." It was done as YHWH commanded Moses.

The Place of Sacrifice

WEDNESDAY Lev 17:1 YHWH spoke to Moses, saying,

Lev 17:2 "Speak to Aaron, and to his sons, and to all the children of Israel, and say to them: 'This is the thing which YHWH has commanded,

Lev 17:3 Whatever man there is of the house of Israel, who kills a bull, or lamb, or goat, in the camp, or who kills it outside the camp,

Lev 17:4 and hasn't brought it to the door of the Tent of Meeting, to offer it as an offering to YHWH before YHWH's tabernacle: blood shall be imputed to that man. He has shed blood; and that man shall be cut off from among his people.

Lev 17:5 This is to the end that the children of Israel may bring their sacrifices, which they sacrifice in the open field, that they may bring them to YHWH, to the door of the Tent of Meeting, to the priest, and sacrifice them for sacrifices of peace offerings to YHWH.

Lev 17:6 The priest shall sprinkle the blood on YHWH's altar at the door of the Tent of Meeting, and burn the fat for a pleasant aroma to YHWH.

Lev 17:7 **They shall no more sacrifice their sacrifices to the goat idols, after which they play the prostitute. This shall be a statute forever to them throughout their generations.'**

THURSDAY Lev 17:8 "You shall say to them, 'Any man there is of the house of Israel, or of the strangers who live as foreigners among them, who offers a burnt offering or sacrifice,

Lev 17:9 and doesn't bring it to the door of the Tent of Meeting, to sacrifice it to YHWH; that man shall be cut off from his people.

Laws Against Eating Blood

Lev 17:10 "'Any man of the house of Israel, or of the strangers who live as foreigners among them, who eats any kind of blood, I will set my face against that soul who eats blood, and will cut him off from among his people.

Lev 17:11 **For the life of the flesh is in the blood; and I have given it to you on the altar to make atonement for your souls: for it is the blood that makes atonement by reason of the life.**

Lev 17:12 Therefore I have said to the children of Israel, "No person among you may eat blood, nor may any stranger who lives as a foreigner among you eat blood."

Lev 17:13 "'Whatever man there is of the children of Israel, or of the strangers who live as foreigners among them, who takes in hunting any animal or bird that may be eaten; he shall pour out its blood, and cover it with dust.

Lev 17:14 For as to the life of all flesh, its blood is with its life: therefore I said to the children of Israel, "You shall not eat the blood of any kind of flesh; for the life of all flesh is its blood. Whoever eats it shall be cut off."

Lev 17:15 "'Every person that eats what dies of itself, or that which is torn by animals, whether he is native-born or a foreigner, he shall wash his clothes, and bathe himself in water, and be unclean until the evening: then he shall be clean.

Lev 17:16 But if he doesn't wash them, or bathe his flesh, then he shall bear his iniquity.'"

Unlawful Sexual Relations

Lev 18:1 YHWH said to Moses,

Lev 18:2 "Speak to the children of Israel, and say to them, 'I am YHWH your God.

Lev 18:3 You shall not do as they do in the land of Egypt, where you lived: and you shall not do as they do in the land of Canaan, where I am bringing you. You shall not follow their statutes.

Lev 18:4 **You shall do my ordinances, and you shall keep my statutes, and walk in them: I am YHWH your God.**

Lev 18:5 You shall therefore keep my statutes and my ordinances; which if a man does, he shall live in them. I am YHWH.

FRIDAY Lev 18:6 *"'None of you shall approach any close relatives, to uncover their nakedness: I am YHWH.*

Lev 18:7 "'You shall not uncover the nakedness of your father, nor the nakedness of your mother: she is your mother. You shall not uncover her nakedness.

Lev 18:8 "'You shall not uncover the nakedness of your father's wife. It is your father's nakedness.

Lev 18:9 "'You shall not uncover the nakedness of your sister, the daughter of your father, or the daughter of your mother, whether born at home, or born abroad.

Lev 18:10 "'You shall not uncover the nakedness of your son's daughter, or of your daughter's daughter, even their nakedness: for theirs is your own nakedness.

Lev 18:11 "'You shall not uncover the nakedness of your father's wife's daughter, conceived by your father, since she is your sister.

Lev 18:12 "'You shall not uncover the nakedness of your father's sister: she is your father's near kinswoman.

Lev 18:13 "'You shall not uncover the nakedness of your mother's sister: for she is your mother's near kinswoman.

Lev 18:14 "'You shall not uncover the nakedness of your father's brother, you shall not approach his wife. She is your aunt.

Lev 18:15 "'You shall not uncover the nakedness of your daughter-in-law: she is your son's wife. You shall not uncover her nakedness.

Lev 18:16 "'You shall not uncover the nakedness of your brother's wife. It is your brother's nakedness.

Lev 18:17 "'You shall not uncover the nakedness of a woman and her daughter. You shall not take her son's daughter, or her daughter's daughter, to uncover her nakedness; they are near kinswomen: it is wickedness.

Lev 18:18 "'You shall not take a wife in addition to her sister, to be a rival, to uncover her nakedness, while her sister is still alive.

Lev 18:19 "'You shall not approach a woman to uncover her nakedness, as long as she is impure by her uncleanness.

Lev 18:20 "'You shall not lie carnally with your neighbor's wife, and defile yourself with her.

Lev 18:21 "'You shall not give any of your children as a sacrifice to Molech. You shall not profane the name of your God. I am YHWH.

SABBATH Lev 18:22 "'You shall not lie with a man, as with a woman. That is detestable.

Lev 18:23 "'You shall not lie with any animal to defile yourself with it. No woman may give herself to an animal, to lie down with it: it is a perversion.

Lev 18:24 "'Don't defile yourselves in any of these things: for in all these the nations which I am casting out before you were defiled.

Lev 18:25 **The land was defiled: therefore I punished its iniquity, and the land vomited out her inhabitants.**

Lev 18:26 You therefore shall keep my statutes and my ordinances, and shall not do any of these abominations; neither the native-born, nor the stranger who lives as a foreigner among you;

Lev 18:27 (for the men of the land that were before you had done all these abominations, and the land became defiled);

Lev 18:28 that the land not vomit you out also, when you defile it, as it vomited out the nation that was before you.

Lev 18:29 "'For whoever shall do any of these abominations, even the souls that do them shall be cut off from among their people.

Lev 18:30 **Therefore you shall keep my requirements, that you do not practice any of these abominable customs, which were practiced before you, and that you do not defile yourselves with them. I am YHWH your God.'"**

MY NOTES

~ EXTRA NOTES ~

VERSE FIND 2 – JOHN 7:7

YOU	L.	HAT	IT	S W	ME,	EST	ES
, B	IT	S A	SE	ORK	HAT	I T	IFY
WO	CAU	AB	RLD	EVI	CA	BE	T E
THE	HA	N'T	IT	OUT	, T	UT	RE

HIDDEN VERSE – MALACHI 4:4

```
E C F O R B E S H O S L D T E
H L H E D A Y C R G O M E L S
I T P I B U R N N E S A T S A
F U R I L N E I A C H S E A N
D A L L C D K T H E O C P R O
U D A N I S R D A P L L A S W
H O W R O R I E A K T W R E I
C K B E D N R D N S E I S S T
E V A L S W I U E L E L B E S
P R O P H E T I L H T U B B L
E A N D T H R E D E A Y T H A
T C O M E P S W I L R L B U R
N T H E M U P Y Q G O Q D M D
L L P X B B L J S X Q W L N W
E N L T U J C K D M O Y F S W
```

APOSTLE
BRIDE
CHILDREN
DISCIPLE
HEIRS
KINGS
PRIEST
PROPHET
RULER
SLAVE
TEACHERS

___, _____, ___ ___ _____, __ _
__ _ _____; ___ ___ ___ _____, ___
___ ___ ___ _____, ____ __
_____; ___ ___ ___ ____ ____
____ ____ ____ __

page 74

KEDOSHIM

קְדֹשִׁים

LEVITICUS

It Means: **Holy Ones**

Our Thirtieth Torah Portion is called Kedoshim! קְדֹשִׁים
Leviticus 19:1 – Leviticus 20:27
PROPHETS: Isaiah 66:1-24; Ezekiel 20:1-20; 22:1-16; Amos 9:7-15
NEW TESTAMENT: Matthew 5:33-37; 43-48; Romans 1:18-32; 13:8-10; Galatians 5:13-26

MAKE A MARK

Each time you hear someone say one of the words below make a "/" beside the word. See how many marks you can get!

evil	
idols	
love	
neighbor	
YHWH	
harvest	

FIRST FIND

~

If someone mentions a verse or scripture that is NOT in this Torah Portion, see if YOU can be the First to Find it!

KEDOSHIM

```
A D U L T E R Y N G R U D G E
U L A E T S E V R A H D M X R
S M O T S U C R Q O A R O L O
S F S K W X G S E C N A L A B
T G N G Y H S N T H G P E K H
R R N A N P G S I H O T C U G
A C R C T I E D S L G L H D I
N U Y H T I N C E E B I Y R E
G R O N O H O A N A R M E A N
E B O L O V E N E A T P U W M
R E V I G R O F V L E H P T B
C U J R E S P E C T G G F O S
Z G B M C P J U D G M E N T P
G S D R A Z I W W I P F D E H
E N O T S J B F G V B J T Q V
```

ADULTERY	HOLY	RESPECT
BALANCES	HONOR	STEAL
CUSTOMS	JUDGMENT	STONE
DEATH	LOVE	STRANGER
FORGIVE	MOLECH	STUMBLING
GLEANINGS	NATION	VENGEANCE
GRUDGE	NEIGHBOR	WEIGHTS
HARVEST	OPPRESS	WIZARDS

Word Search Created by Torah Town

YHWH Is Holy

SUNDAY Lev 19:1 YHWH spoke to Moses, saying,

Lev 19:2 **"Speak to all the congregation of the children of Israel, and tell them, 'You shall be holy; for I, YHWH your God, am holy.**

Lev 19:3 "'Each one of you shall respect his mother and his father. You shall keep my Sabbaths. I am YHWH your God.

Lev 19:4 "'Don't turn to idols, nor make molten gods for yourselves. I am YHWH your God.

Lev 19:5 "'When you offer a sacrifice of peace offerings to YHWH, you shall offer it so that you may be accepted.

Lev 19:6 It shall be eaten the same day you offer it, and on the next day: and if anything remains until the third day, it shall be burned with fire.

Lev 19:7 If it is eaten at all on the third day, it is an abomination. It will not be accepted;

Lev 19:8 but everyone who eats it shall bear his iniquity, because he has profaned the holy thing of YHWH, and that soul shall be cut off from his people.

Love Your Neighbor as Yourself

Lev 19:9 "'When you reap the harvest of your land, you shall not wholly reap the corners of your field, neither shall you gather the gleanings of your harvest.

Lev 19:10 You shall not glean your vineyard, neither shall you gather the fallen grapes of your vineyard. You shall leave them for the poor and for the foreigner. I am YHWH your God.

Lev 19:11 **"'You shall not steal. "'You shall not lie. "'You shall not deceive one another.**

Lev 19:12 **"'You shall not swear by my name falsely, and profane the name of your God. I am YHWH.**

Lev 19:13 **"'You shall not oppress your neighbor, nor rob him. "'The wages of a hired servant shall not remain with you all night until the morning.**

Lev 19:14 **"'You shall not curse the deaf, nor put a stumbling block before the blind; but you shall fear your God. I am YHWH.**

MONDAY Lev 19:15 "'You shall do no injustice in judgment. You shall not be partial to the poor, nor show favoritism to the great; but you shall judge your neighbor in righteousness.

Lev 19:16 "'You shall not go up and down as a slanderer among your people. "'You shall not endanger the life of your neighbor. I am YHWH.

Lev 19:17 *"'You shall not hate your brother in your heart. You shall surely rebuke your neighbor, and not bear sin because of him.*

Lev 19:18 "'You shall not take vengeance, nor bear any grudge against the children of your people; but you shall love your neighbor as yourself. I am YHWH.

You Shall Keep My Statutes

Lev 19:19 "'You shall keep my statutes. "'You shall not crossbreed different kinds of animals. "'You shall not sow your field with two kinds of seed; "'Don't wear a garment made of two kinds of material.

Lev 19:20 "'If a man lies carnally with a woman who is a slave girl, pledged to be married to another man, and not ransomed, or given her freedom; they shall be punished. They shall not be put to death, because she was not free.

Lev 19:21 He shall bring his trespass offering to YHWH, to the door of the Tent of Meeting, even a ram for a trespass offering.

Lev 19:22 The priest shall make atonement for him with the ram of the trespass offering before YHWH for his sin which he has committed: and the sin which he has committed shall be forgiven him.

TUESDAY Lev 19:23 "When you come into the land, and have planted all kinds of trees for food, then you shall count their fruit as forbidden. Three years they shall be forbidden to you. It shall not be eaten.

Lev 19:24 *But in the fourth year all its fruit shall be holy, for giving praise to YHWH.*

Lev 19:25 In the fifth year you shall eat its fruit, that it may yield its increase to you. I am YHWH your God.

Lev 19:26 *"'You shall not eat any meat with the blood still in it. You shall not use enchantments, nor practice sorcery.*

Lev 19:27 "'You shall not cut the hair on the sides of your head or clip off the edge of your beard.

Lev 19:28 *"'You shall not make any cuttings in your flesh for the dead, nor tattoo any marks on you. I am YHWH.*

Lev 19:29 "'Don't profane your daughter, to make her a prostitute; lest the land fall to prostitution, and the land become full of wickedness.

Lev 19:30 *"'You shall keep my Sabbaths, and reverence my sanctuary; I am YHWH.*

Lev 19:31 "'Don't turn to those who are mediums, nor to the wizards. Don't seek them out, to be defiled by them. I am YHWH your God.

Lev 19:32 *"'You shall rise up before the gray head, and honor the face of an old man, and you shall fear your God. I am YHWH.*

WEDNESDAY Lev 19:33 "'If a stranger lives as a foreigner with you in your land, you shall not do him wrong.

Lev 19:34 The stranger who lives as a foreigner with you shall be to you as the native-born among you, and you shall love him as yourself; for you lived as foreigners in the land of Egypt. I am YHWH your God.

Lev 19:35 "'You shall do no unrighteousness in judgment, in measures of length, of weight, or of quantity.

Lev 19:36 You shall have just balances, just weights, a just ephah, and a just hin. I am YHWH your God, who brought you out of the land of Egypt.

Lev 19:37 *"'You shall observe all my statutes, and all my ordinances, and do them. I am YHWH.'"*

Punishment for Child Sacrifice

THURSDAY Lev 20:1 YHWH spoke to Moses, saying,

Lev 20:2 "Moreover, you shall tell the children of Israel, 'Anyone of the children of Israel, or of the strangers who live as foreigners in Israel, who gives any of his offspring to Molech; he shall surely be put to death. The people of the land shall stone him with stones.

Lev 20:3 I also will set my face against that person, and will cut him off from among his people because he has given of his offspring to Molech, to defile my sanctuary, and to profane my holy name.

Lev 20:4 If the people of the land all hide their eyes from that person, when he gives of his offspring to Molech, and don't put him to death;

Lev 20:5 then I will set my face against that man, and against his family, and will cut him off, and all who play the prostitute after him, to play the prostitute with Molech, from among their people.

Lev 20:6 "'The person that turns to those who are mediums, and to the wizards, to play the prostitute after them, I will even set my face against that person, and will cut him off from among his people.

Lev 20:7 *"'Sanctify yourselves therefore, and be holy; for I am YHWH your God.*

FRIDAY Lev 20:8 You shall keep my statutes, and do them. I am YHWH who sanctifies you.

Lev 20:9 **"'For everyone who curses his father or his mother shall surely be put to death: he has cursed his father or his mother; his blood shall be upon him.**

Punishments for Sexual Immorality

Lev 20:10 "'The man who commits adultery with another man's wife, even he who commits adultery with his neighbor's wife, the adulterer and the adulteress shall surely be put to death.

Lev 20:11 "'The man who lies with his father's wife has uncovered his father's nakedness: both of them shall surely be put to death; their blood shall be upon them.

Lev 20:12 "'If a man lies with his daughter-in-law, both of them shall surely be put to death: they have committed a perversion; their blood shall be upon them.

Lev 20:13 "'If a man lies with a male, as with a woman, both of them have committed an abomination: they shall surely be put to death; their blood shall be upon them.

Lev 20:14 "'If a man takes a wife and her mother, it is wickedness: they shall be burned with fire, both he and they; that there may be no wickedness among you.

Lev 20:15 "'If a man lies with an animal, he shall surely be put to death; and you shall kill the animal.

Lev 20:16 "'If a woman approaches any animal, and lies with it, you shall kill the woman and the animal. They shall surely be put to death. Their blood shall be upon them.

Lev 20:17 "'If a man takes his sister, his father's daughter, or his mother's daughter, and sees her nakedness, and she sees his nakedness; it is a shameful thing. They shall be cut off in the sight of the children of their people. He has uncovered his sister's nakedness. He shall bear his iniquity.

Lev 20:18 "'If a man lies with a woman having her monthly period, and uncovers her nakedness; he has made naked her fountain, and she has uncovered the fountain of her blood. Both of them shall be cut off from among their people.

Lev 20:19 "'You shall not uncover the nakedness of your mother's sister, nor of your father's sister; for he has made his close relative naked. They shall bear their iniquity.

Lev 20:20 If a man lies with his uncle's wife, he has uncovered his uncle's nakedness. They shall bear their sin. They shall die childless.

Lev 20:21 "'If a man takes his brother's wife, it is an impurity. He has uncovered his brother's nakedness. They shall be childless.

You Shall Be Holy

Lev 20:22 *"'You shall therefore keep all my statutes, and all my ordinances, and do them; that the land, where I am bringing you to dwell, may not vomit you out.*

<u>SABBATH</u> Lev 20:23 *You shall not walk in the customs of the nation, which I am casting out before you: for they did all these things, and therefore I abhorred them.*

Lev 20:24 But I have said to you, "You shall inherit their land, and I will give it to you to possess it, a land flowing with milk and honey." I am YHWH your God, who has separated you from the peoples.

Lev 20:25 "'You shall therefore make a distinction between the clean animal and the unclean, and between the unclean fowl and the clean: and you shall not make yourselves abominable by animal, or by bird, or by anything with which the ground teems, which I have separated from you as unclean for you.

Lev 20:26 You shall be holy to me; for I, YHWH, am holy, and have set you apart from the peoples, that you should be mine.

Lev 20:27 "'A man or a woman that is a medium, or is a wizard, shall surely be put to death: they shall stone them with stones. Their blood shall be upon them.'"

MY NOTES

~ EXTRA NOTES ~

SCRAMBLE – EZEKIEL 20:6

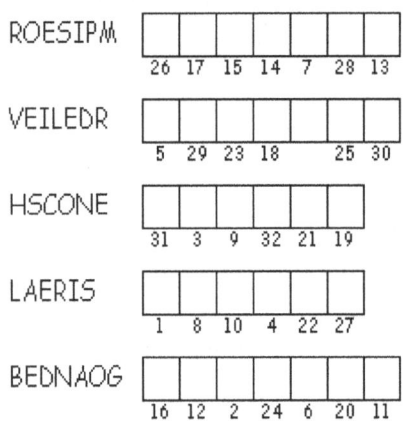

VERSE FIND – HEBREWS 13:4

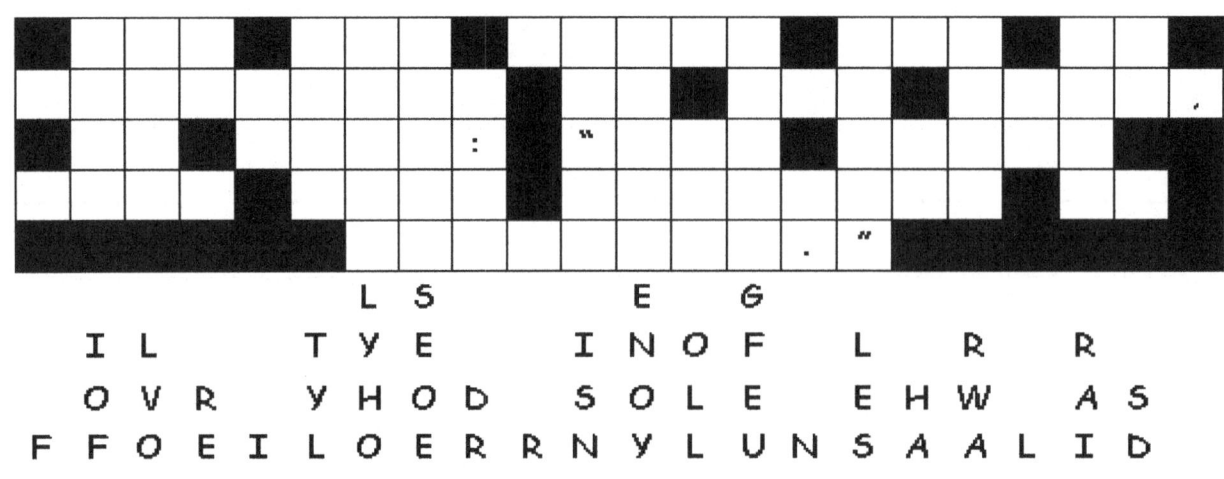

EMOR
אֱמֹר
LEVITICUS

It Means: **Speak Gently**

Our Thirty-first Torah Portion is called Emor! אֱמֹר
Leviticus 21:1 – Leviticus 24:23

PROPHETS: 1 Samuel 15:2-34; Ezekiel 44:15-31; Zechariah 14:16-21; Malachi
NEW TESTAMENT: Matthew 25:1-13; Mark 2:20-3:5; Luke 12:1-59; Acts 20:6-16; Romans 11:11-36; 1 Corinthians 5:1-8; Galatians 3:23-29; Ephesians 2; 5:25-27; 1 Thessalonians 5:1-11; 1 Peter 2:1-10; 2 Peter 3:13-18; Revelation 21

MAKE A MARK

Each time you hear someone say one of the words below make a '/" beside the word. See how many marks you can get!

sabbath	
passover	
trumpets	
weeks	
eat	
offering	

FIRST FIND

~

If someone mentions a verse or scripture that is NOT in this Torah Portion, see if YOU can be the First to Find it!

EMOR

```
R E T H G U A D S A B B A T H
N L E T U T I T S O R P Z F D
X O N Q A E V C U T T I N G S
T H I S A C C E P T A B L E W
S B T T E V A L S H Z S G O P
O S C F P U K S B F T B V D A
C T E M R U T N Q I O I E E S
E S F A X E R S U C B N H N S
T A E I P D E R H O K J O E O
N E D M Y P F W O A P U L V V
E F U E L T G T I C V R I A E
P R K D S O H U I L Q E N E R
T A E R Y S K E D W L D E L P
H U I T N E M E N O T A S N G
M F V G N I R P S F F O S U X
```

ACCEPTABLE	FEASTS	PENTECOST
ATONEMENT	FIRSTFRUITS	PROSTITUTE
BOOTHS	FREEWILL	SABBATH
CORRUPTION	HOLINESS	SHAVE
CUTTINGS	INJURED	SLAVE
DAUGHTER	MAIMED	TRUMPETS
DEFECT	OFFSPRING	UNLEAVENED
EAT	PASSOVER	VOW

Word Search Created by Torah Town

Command the children of Israel, that they bring to you pure olive oil beaten for the light, to cause a lamp to burn continually.

Holiness and the Priests

SUNDAY Lev 21:1 YHWH said to Moses, "Speak to the priests, the sons of Aaron, and say to them, 'A priest shall not defile himself for the dead among his people;

Lev 21:2 except for his relatives that are near to him: for his mother, for his father, for his son, for his daughter, for his brother,

Lev 21:3 and for his virgin sister who is near to him, who has had no husband; for her he may defile himself.

Lev 21:4 ***He shall not defile himself, being a chief man among his people, to profane himself.***

Lev 21:5 "'They shall not shave their heads or shave off the corners of their beards or make any cuttings in their flesh.

Lev 21:6 They shall be holy to their God, and not profane the name of their God; for they offer the offerings of YHWH made by fire, the bread of their God; therefore they shall be holy.

Lev 21:7 "'They shall not marry a woman who is a prostitute, or profane. They shall not marry a woman divorced from her husband; for he is holy to his God.

Lev 21:8 You shall sanctify him therefore; for he offers the bread of your God. He shall be holy to you; for I YHWH, who sanctify you, am holy.

Lev 21:9 ***"'The daughter of any priest, if she profanes herself by playing the prostitute, she profanes her father. She shall be burned with fire.***

Lev 21:10 "'He who is the high priest among his brothers, upon whose head the anointing oil is poured, and that is consecrated to put on the garments, shall not let the hair of his head hang loose, or tear his clothes.

Lev 21:11 He must not go in to any dead body, or defile himself for his father, or for his mother.

Lev 21:12 He shall not go out of the sanctuary, nor profane the sanctuary of his God; for the crown of the anointing oil of his God is upon him. I am YHWH.

Lev 21:13 "'He shall take a wife in her virginity.

Lev 21:14 A widow, or one divorced, or a woman who has been defiled, or a prostitute, these he shall not marry: but a virgin of his own people shall he take as a wife.

Lev 21:15 He shall not profane his offspring among his people, for I am YHWH who sanctifies him.'"

MONDAY Lev 21:16 YHWH spoke to Moses, saying,

Lev 21:17 "Say to Aaron, 'None of your offspring throughout their generations who has a defect may approach to offer the bread of his God.

Lev 21:18 For whatever man he is that has a defect, he shall not draw near: a blind man, or a lame, or he who has a flat nose, or any deformity,

Lev 21:19 or a man who has an injured foot, or an injured hand,

Lev 21:20 or hunchbacked, or a dwarf, or one who has a defect in his eye, or an itching disease, or scabs, or who has damaged testicles.

Lev 21:21 No man of the offspring of Aaron the priest who has a defect shall come near to offer the offerings of YHWH made by fire. Since he has a defect, he shall not come near to offer the bread of his God.

Lev 21:22 **He shall eat the bread of his God, both of the most holy, and of the holy.**

Lev 21:23 He shall not come near to the veil, nor come near to the altar, because he has a defect; that he may not profane my sanctuaries, for I am YHWH who sanctifies them.'"

Lev 21:24 So Moses spoke to Aaron, and to his sons, and to all the children of Israel.

Lev 22:1 YHWH spoke to Moses, saying,

Lev 22:2 "Tell Aaron and his sons to separate themselves from the holy things of the children of Israel, which they make holy to me, and that they not profane my holy name. I am YHWH.

Lev 22:3 "Tell them, 'If anyone of all your offspring throughout your generations approaches the holy things, which the children of Israel make holy to YHWH, having his uncleanness on him, that soul shall be cut off from before me. I am YHWH.

Lev 22:4 "'Whoever of the offspring of Aaron is a leper or has an issue; he shall not eat of the holy things, until he is clean. Whoever touches anything that is unclean by the dead, or a man whose offspring goes from him;

Lev 22:5 or whoever touches any creeping thing, whereby he may be made unclean, or a man of whom he may take uncleanness, whatever uncleanness he has;

Lev 22:6 the person that touches any such shall be unclean until the evening, and shall not eat of the holy things, unless he bathes his body in water.

Lev 22:7 When the sun is down, he shall be clean; and afterward he shall eat of the holy things, because it is his bread.

Lev 22:8 *That which dies of itself, or is torn by animals, he shall not eat, defiling himself by it. I am YHWH.*

Lev 22:9 "'They shall therefore follow my commandment, lest they bear sin for it, and die therein, if they profane it. I am YHWH who sanctifies them.

Lev 22:10 "'No stranger shall eat of the holy thing: a foreigner living with the priests, or a hired servant, shall not eat of the holy thing.

Lev 22:11 But if a priest buys a slave, purchased by his money, he shall eat of it; and such as are born in his house, they shall eat of his bread.

Lev 22:12 If a priest's daughter is married to an outsider, she shall not eat of the heave offering of the holy things.

Lev 22:13 But if a priest's daughter is a widow, or divorced, and has no child, and has returned to her father's house, as in her youth, she may eat of her father's bread: but no stranger shall eat any of it.

Lev 22:14 "'If a man eats something holy unwittingly, then he shall add the fifth part of its value to it, and shall give the holy thing to the priest.

Lev 22:15 The priests shall not profane the holy things of the children of Israel, which they offer to YHWH,

Lev 22:16 and so cause them to bear the iniquity that brings guilt, when they eat their holy things; for I am YHWH who sanctifies them.'"

Acceptable Offerings

TUESDAY Lev 22:17 YHWH spoke to Moses, saying,

Lev 22:18 "Speak to Aaron, and to his sons, and to all the children of Israel, and say to them, 'Whoever is of the house of Israel, or of the foreigners in Israel, who offers his offering, whether it is any of their vows, or any of their freewill offerings, which they offer to YHWH for a burnt offering;

Lev 22:19 that you may be accepted, you shall offer a male without defect, of the bulls, of the sheep, or of the goats.

Lev 22:20 But whatever has a defect, that you shall not offer; for it shall not be acceptable for you.

Lev 22:21 *Whoever offers a sacrifice of peace offerings to YHWH to accomplish a vow, or for a freewill offering, of the herd or of the flock, it shall be perfect to be accepted. It shall have no defect.*

Lev 22:22 Blind, injured, maimed, having a wart, festering, or having a running sore: you shall not offer these to YHWH, nor make an offering by fire of them on the altar to YHWH.

Lev 22:23 Either a bull or a lamb that has any deformity or lacking in his parts, that you may offer for a freewill offering; but for a vow it shall not be accepted.

Lev 22:24 You must not offer to YHWH that which has its testicles bruised, crushed, broken, or cut. You must not do this in your land.

Lev 22:25 You must not offer the bread of your God from the hand of a foreigner as any of these; because their corruption is in them. There is a defect in them. They shall not be accepted for you.'"

Lev 22:26 YHWH spoke to Moses, saying,

Lev 22:27 "When a bull, or a sheep, or a goat, is born, then it shall remain seven days with its mother; and from the eighth day and thenceforth it shall be accepted for the offering of an offering made by fire to YHWH.

Lev 22:28 Whether it is a cow or ewe, you shall not kill it and its young both in one day.

Lev 22:29 *"When you sacrifice a sacrifice of thanksgiving to YHWH, you shall sacrifice it so that you may be accepted.*

Lev 22:30 It shall be eaten on the same day; you shall leave none of it until the morning. I am YHWH.

Lev 22:31 "Therefore you shall keep my commandments, and do them. I am YHWH.

Lev 22:32 You shall not profane my holy name, but I will be made holy among the children of Israel. I am YHWH who makes you holy,

Lev 22:33 who brought you out of the land of Egypt, to be your God. I am YHWH."

Feasts of YHWH

WEDNESDAY Lev 23:1 YHWH spoke to Moses, saying,

Lev 23:2 "Speak to the children of Israel, and tell them, 'The set feasts of YHWH, which you shall proclaim to be holy convocations, even these are my set feasts.

The Sabbath

Lev 23:3 *"'Six days shall work be done, but on the seventh day is a Sabbath of solemn rest, a holy convocation; you shall do no kind of work. It is a Sabbath to YHWH in all your dwellings.*

The Passover

Lev 23:4 "'These are the set feasts of YHWH, even holy convocations, which you shall proclaim in their appointed season.

Lev 23:5 **In the first month, on the fourteenth day of the month in the evening, is YHWH's Passover.**

Lev 23:6 **On the fifteenth day of the same month is the feast of unleavened bread to YHWH. Seven days you shall eat unleavened bread.**

Lev 23:7 In the first day you shall have a holy convocation. You shall do no regular work.

Lev 23:8 But you shall offer an offering made by fire to YHWH seven days. In the seventh day is a holy convocation: you shall do no regular work.'"

The Feast of Firstfruits

Lev 23:9 YHWH spoke to Moses, saying,

Lev 23:10 "Speak to the children of Israel, and tell them, 'When you have come into the land which I give to you, and shall reap its harvest, then you shall bring the sheaf of the first fruits of your harvest to the priest:

Lev 23:11 **and he shall wave the sheaf before YHWH, to be accepted for you. On the next day after the Sabbath the priest shall wave it.**

Lev 23:12 On the day when you wave the sheaf, you shall offer a male lamb without defect a year old for a burnt offering to YHWH.

Lev 23:13 The meal offering with it shall be two tenths of an ephah of fine flour mingled with oil, an offering made by fire to YHWH for a pleasant aroma; and the drink offering with it shall be of wine, the fourth part of a hin.

Lev 23:14 You must not eat bread, or roasted grain, or fresh grain, until this same day, until you have brought the offering of your God. This is a statute forever throughout your generations in all your dwellings.

The Feast of Weeks

Lev 23:15 "'You shall count from the next day after the Sabbath, from the day that you brought the sheaf of the wave offering; seven Sabbaths shall be completed:

Lev 23:16 **even to the next day after the seventh Sabbath you shall count fifty days; and you shall offer a new meal offering to YHWH.**

Lev 23:17 You shall bring out of your habitations two loaves of bread for a wave offering made of two tenths of an ephah of fine flour. They shall be baked with yeast, for first fruits to YHWH.

Lev 23:18 You shall present with the bread seven lambs without defect a year old, one young bull, and two rams. They shall be a burnt offering to YHWH, with their meal offering, and their drink offerings, even an offering made by fire, of a sweet aroma to YHWH.

Lev 23:19 You shall offer one male goat for a sin offering, and two male lambs a year old for a sacrifice of peace offerings.

Lev 23:20 The priest shall wave them with the bread of the first fruits for a wave offering before YHWH, with the two lambs. They shall be holy to YHWH for the priest.

Lev 23:21 You shall make proclamation on the same day: there shall be a holy convocation to you; you shall do no regular work. This is a statute forever in all your dwellings throughout your generations.

Lev 23:22 "'When you reap the harvest of your land, you must not wholly reap into the corners of your field, and you must not gather the gleanings of your harvest. You must leave them for the poor, and for the foreigner. I am YHWH your God.'"

The Feast of Trumpets

<u>THURSDAY</u> Lev 23:23 YHWH spoke to Moses, saying,

Lev 23:24 *"Speak to the children of Israel, saying, 'In the seventh month, on the first day of the month, shall be a solemn rest to you, a memorial of blowing of trumpets, a holy convocation.*

Lev 23:25 You shall do no regular work; and you shall offer an offering made by fire to YHWH.'"

The Day of Atonement

Lev 23:26 YHWH spoke to Moses, saying,

Lev 23:27 *"However on the tenth day of this seventh month is the day of atonement: it shall be a holy convocation to you, and you shall afflict yourselves; and you shall offer an offering made by fire to YHWH.*

Lev 23:28 You shall do no kind of work in that same day; for it is a day of atonement, to make atonement for you before YHWH your God.

Lev 23:29 *For whoever it is who shall not deny himself in that same day; shall be cut off from his people.*

Lev 23:30 Whoever it is who does any kind of work in that same day, that person I will destroy from among his people.

Lev 23:31 You shall do no kind of work: it is a statute forever throughout your generations in all your dwellings.

Lev 23:32 It shall be a Sabbath of solemn rest for you, and you shall deny yourselves. In the ninth day of the month at evening, from evening to evening, you shall keep your Sabbath."

The Feast of Booths

FRIDAY Lev 23:33 YHWH spoke to Moses, saying,

Lev 23:34 **"Speak to the children of Israel, and say, 'On the fifteenth day of this seventh month is the feast of tents for seven days to YHWH.**

Lev 23:35 On the first day shall be a holy convocation: you shall do no regular work.

Lev 23:36 Seven days you shall offer an offering made by fire to YHWH. On the eighth day shall be a holy convocation to you; and you shall offer an offering made by fire to YHWH. It is a solemn assembly; you shall do no regular work.

Lev 23:37 "'These are the appointed feasts of YHWH, which you shall proclaim to be holy convocations, to offer an offering made by fire to YHWH, a burnt offering, and a meal offering, a sacrifice, and drink offerings, each on its own day—

Lev 23:38 in addition to the Sabbaths of YHWH, and in addition to your gifts, and in addition to all your vows, and in addition to all your freewill offerings, which you give to YHWH.

Lev 23:39 "'So on the fifteenth day of the seventh month, when you have gathered in the fruits of the land, you shall keep the feast of YHWH seven days: on the first day shall be a solemn rest, and on the eighth day shall be a solemn rest.

Lev 23:40 You shall take on the first day the fruit of goodly trees, branches of palm trees, and boughs of thick trees, and willows of the brook; and you shall rejoice before YHWH your God seven days.

Lev 23:41 **You shall keep it as a feast to YHWH seven days in the year. It is a statute forever throughout your generations. You shall keep it in the seventh month.**

Lev 23:42 You shall dwell in temporary shelters for seven days. All who are native-born in Israel shall dwell in temporary shelters,

Lev 23:43 that your generations may know that I made the children of Israel to dwell in temporary shelters, when I brought them out of the land of Egypt. I am YHWH your God.'"

Lev 23:44 Moses declared to the children of Israel the appointed feasts of YHWH.

The Lamps

<u>SABBATH</u> Lev 24:1 YHWH spoke to Moses, saying,

Lev 24:2 "Command the children of Israel, that they bring to you pure olive oil beaten for the light, to cause a lamp to burn continually.

Lev 24:3 Outside of the veil of the Testimony, in the Tent of Meeting, shall Aaron keep it in order from evening to morning before YHWH continually: it shall be a statute forever throughout your generations.

Lev 24:4 **He shall keep in order the lamps on the pure gold lamp stand before YHWH continually.**

Bread for the Tabernacle

Lev 24:5 "You shall take fine flour, and bake twelve cakes of it: two tenths of an ephah shall be in one cake.

Lev 24:6 You shall set them in two rows, six on a row, on the pure gold table before YHWH.

Lev 24:7 You shall put pure frankincense on each row, that it may be to the bread for a memorial, even an offering made by fire to YHWH.

Lev 24:8 **Every Sabbath day he shall set it in order before YHWH continually. It is an everlasting covenant on the behalf of the children of Israel.**

Lev 24:9 It shall be for Aaron and his sons; and they shall eat it in a holy place: for it is most holy to him of the offerings of YHWH made by fire by a perpetual statute."

Punishment for Blasphemy

Lev 24:10 The son of an Israelite woman, whose father was an Egyptian, went out among the children of Israel; and the son of the Israelite woman and a man of Israel strove together in the camp.

Lev 24:11 The son of the Israelite woman blasphemed the Name, and cursed; and they brought him to Moses. His mother's name was Shelomith, the daughter of Dibri, of the tribe of Dan.

Lev 24:12 They put him in custody, until YHWH's will should be declared to them.

Lev 24:13 YHWH spoke to Moses, saying,

Lev 24:14 "Bring out of the camp him who cursed; and let all who heard him lay their hands on his head, and let all the congregation stone him.

Lev 24:15 **You shall speak to the children of Israel, saying, 'Whoever curses his God shall bear his sin.**

Lev 24:16 He who blasphemes YHWH's name, he shall surely be put to death. All the congregation shall certainly stone him. The foreigner as well as the native-born, when he blasphemes the Name, shall be put to death.

An Eye for an Eye

Lev 24:17 **"'He who strikes any man mortally shall surely be put to death.**

Lev 24:18 He who strikes an animal mortally shall make it good, life for life.

Lev 24:19 If anyone injures his neighbor; as he has done, so shall it be done to him:

Lev 24:20 fracture for fracture, eye for eye, tooth for tooth; as he has injured someone, so shall it be done to him.

Lev 24:21 He who kills an animal shall make it good; and he who kills a man shall be put to death.

Lev 24:22 You shall have one kind of law for the foreigner as well as the native-born; for I am YHWH your God.'"

Lev 24:23 Moses spoke to the children of Israel; and they brought him who had cursed out of the camp, and stoned him with stones. The children of Israel did as YHWH commanded Moses.

MY NOTES

~ EXTRA NOTES ~

SCRAMBLE – 1 SAMUEL 15:1

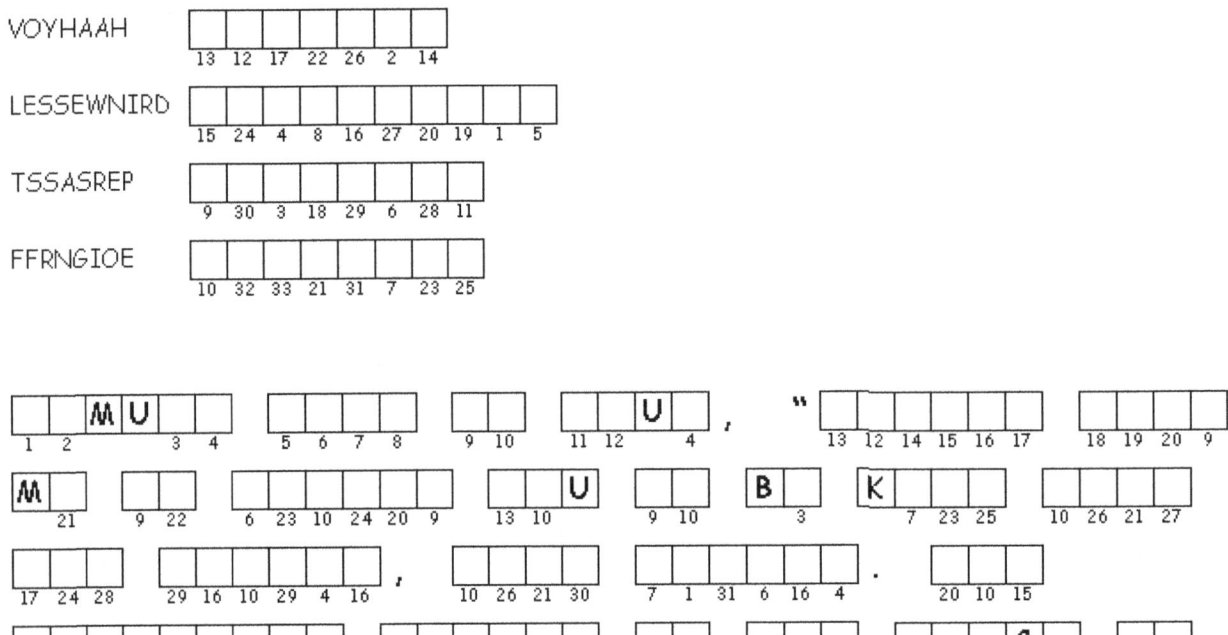

VERSE FIND 2 – EPHESIANS 2:10

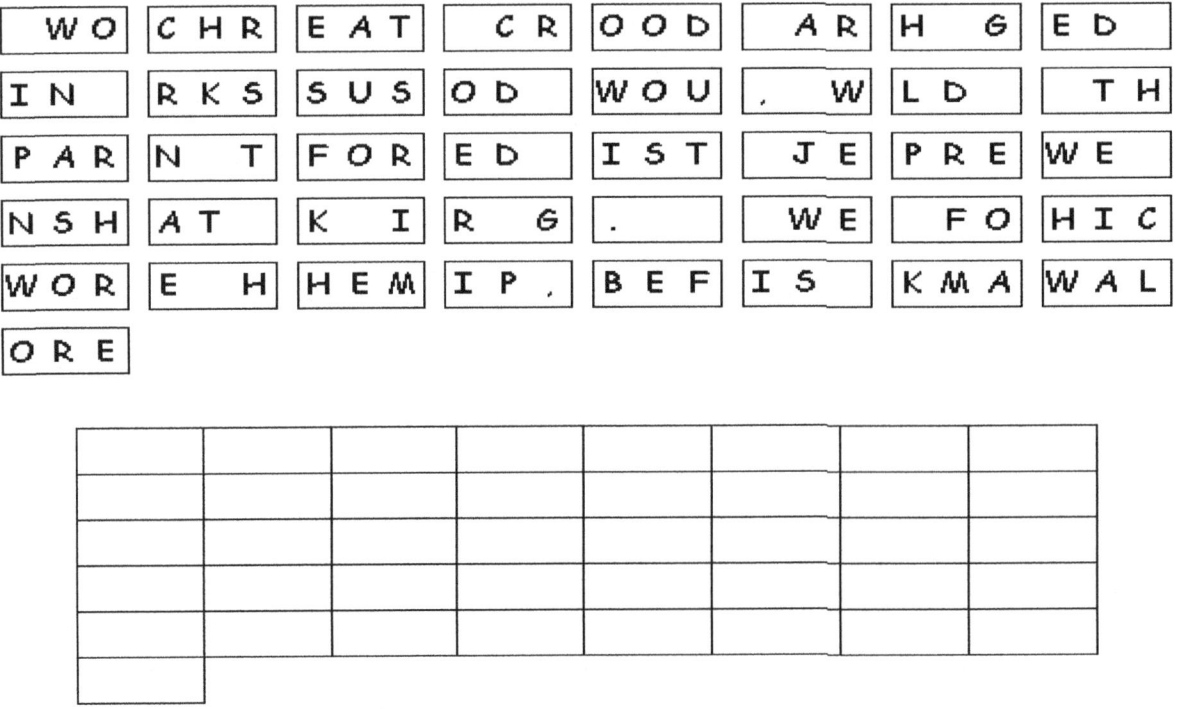

BEHAR
בְּהַר
LEVITICUS

It Means: **On The Mount**

Our Thirty-Second Torah Portion is called Behar! בְּהַר

Leviticus 25:1 – Leviticus 26:2

PROPHETS: Jeremiah 32:6-27;

NEW TESTAMENT: Luke 4:16-21; 1 Corinthians 7:21-24; Galatians 6:7-10

MAKE A MARK

Each time you hear someone say one of the words below make a '/" beside the word. See how many marks you can get!

children	
jubilee	
fields	
years	
count	
feasts	

FIRST FIND

~

If someone mentions a verse or scripture that is NOT in this Torah Portion, see if YOU can be the First to Find it!

BEHAR

```
J Y T R E P O R P L O D I N L
V H T K S M T N E D I S E R E
I O S S E N D N I K H B R C V
N U E W F V Q M H T N A H E I
E S V V J Z J A E O L I Q O T
Y E R J W U R I I I L N J A E
A S A I B S T T E D W T J N S
R G H I H F P N R O F E K W Q
D J L N I M T E H N K R O B M
R E E F E C N A T I R E H N I
E S Y D T I F O R P D S A B N
S H E Q C P A E R N L T S T X
I R F I E L D S A N U M B E R
R A T S E G A L L I V E J P P
J Y W D R G B L E S S I N G S
```

ALIEN	HOUSES	NUMBER
BLESSINGS	IDOL	PROFIT
CHILDREN	INHERITANCE	PROPERTY
CITY	INTEREST	REAP
FIELDS	JUBILEE	REDEMPTION
FIFTIETH	KINDNESS	RESIDENT
HARSHNESS	LAND	VILLAGES
HARVEST	LEVITES	VINEYARD

Word Search Created by Torah Town

Biblical Feasts

FIRST MONTH - NISSAN/AVIV	50 DAYS LATER	SEVENTH MONTH - TISHREI
Feast #1 Passover Pesach Lev. 23:5 / Feast #2 Unleavened Bread Lev. 23:6-8 / Feast #3 First Fruits Lev. 23:10-14	Feast #4 Shavuot - Pentecost Lev. 23:16-22	Feast #5 Yom Teruah Trumpets Lev. 23:24-25 / Feast #6 Yom Kippur Atonement Lev. 23:27-32 / Feast #7 Sukkot Tabernacles Lev. 23:34-43
SPRING FEASTS OF YHWH		**FALL FEASTS OF YHWH**

page 102

The Sabbath Year

<u>**SUNDAY**</u> Lev 25:1 YHWH said to Moses in Mount Sinai,

Lev 25:2 "Speak to the children of Israel, and tell them, 'When you come into the land which I give you, then the land shall keep a Sabbath to YHWH.

Lev 25:3 ***You shall sow your field six years, and you shall prune your vineyard six years, and gather in its fruits;***

Lev 25:4 ***but in the seventh year there shall be a Sabbath of solemn rest for the land, a Sabbath to YHWH. You shall not sow your field or prune your vineyard.***

Lev 25:5 What grows of itself in your harvest you shall not reap, and you shall not gather the grapes of your undressed vine. It shall be a year of solemn rest for the land.

Lev 25:6 The Sabbath of the land shall be for food for you; for yourself, for your servant, for your maid, for your hired servant, and for your stranger, who lives as a foreigner with you.

Lev 25:7 For your livestock also, and for the animals that are in your land, shall all its increase be for food.

The Year of Jubilee

Lev 25:8 "'You shall count off seven Sabbaths of years, seven times seven years; and there shall be to you the days of seven Sabbaths of years, even forty-nine years.

Lev 25:9 Then you shall sound the loud trumpet on the tenth day of the seventh month. On the Day of Atonement you shall sound the trumpet throughout all your land.

Lev 25:10 You shall make the fiftieth year holy, and proclaim liberty throughout the land to all its inhabitants. It shall be a jubilee to you; and each of you shall return to his own property, and each of you shall return to his family.

Lev 25:11 ***That fiftieth year shall be a jubilee to you. In it you shall not sow, neither reap that which grows of itself, nor gather from the undressed vines.***

Lev 25:12 For it is a jubilee; it shall be holy to you. You shall eat of its increase out of the field.

Lev 25:13 "'In this Year of Jubilee each of you shall return to his property.

<u>**MONDAY**</u> Lev 25:14 "'If you sell anything to your neighbor, or buy from your neighbor, you shall not wrong one another.

Lev 25:15 According to the number of years after the Jubilee you shall buy from your neighbor. According to the number of years of the crops he shall sell to you.

Lev 25:16 According to the length of the years you shall increase its price, and according to the shortness of the years you shall diminish its price; for he is selling the number of the crops to you.

Lev 25:17 **You shall not wrong one another; but you shall fear your God: for I am YHWH your God.**

Lev 25:18 "'Therefore you shall do my statutes, and keep my ordinances and do them; and you shall dwell in the land in safety.

TUESDAY Lev 25:19 The land shall yield its fruit, and you shall eat your fill, and dwell therein in safety.

Lev 25:20 **If you said, "What shall we eat the seventh year? Behold, we shall not sow, nor gather in our increase;"**

Lev 25:21 then I will command my blessing on you in the sixth year, and it shall bear fruit for the three years.

Lev 25:22 You shall sow the eighth year, and eat of the fruits, the old store; until the ninth year, until its fruits come in, you shall eat the old store.

Redemption of Property

Lev 25:23 "'The land shall not be sold in perpetuity, for the land is mine; for you are strangers and live as foreigners with me.

Lev 25:24 In all the land of your possession you shall grant a redemption for the land.

WEDNESDAY Lev 25:25 **"'If your brother becomes poor, and sells some of his possessions, then his kinsman who is next to him shall come, and redeem that which his brother has sold.**

Lev 25:26 If a man has no one to redeem it, and he becomes prosperous and finds sufficient means to redeem it;

Lev 25:27 then let him reckon the years since its sale, and restore the surplus to the man to whom he sold it; and he shall return to his property.

Lev 25:28 But if he isn't able to get it back for himself, then what he has sold shall remain in the hand of him who has bought it until the Year of Jubilee: and in the Jubilee it shall be released, and he shall return to his property.

THURSDAY Lev 25:29 "'If a man sells a dwelling house in a walled city, then he may redeem it within a whole year after it has been sold. For a full year he shall have the right of redemption.

Lev 25:30 If it isn't redeemed within the space of a full year, then the house that is in the walled city shall be made sure in perpetuity to him who bought it, throughout his generations. It shall not be released in the Jubilee.

Lev 25:31 But the houses of the villages which have no wall around them shall be accounted for with the fields of the country: they may be redeemed, and they shall be released in the Jubilee.

Lev 25:32 *'"Nevertheless the cities of the Levites, the houses in the cities of their possession, the Levites may redeem at any time.*

Lev 25:33 The Levites may redeem the house that was sold, and the city of his possession, and it shall be released in the Jubilee; for the houses of the cities of the Levites are their possession among the children of Israel.

Lev 25:34 But the field of the pasture lands of their cities may not be sold; for it is their perpetual possession.

Kindness for Poor Brothers

Lev 25:35 *"'If your brother has become poor, and his hand can't support himself among you; then you shall uphold him. He shall live with you like an alien and a temporary resident.*

Lev 25:36 Take no interest from him or profit, but fear your God; that your brother may live among you.

Lev 25:37 You shall not lend him your money at interest, nor give him your food for profit.

Lev 25:38 I am YHWH your God, who brought you out of the land of Egypt, to give you the land of Canaan, and to be your God.

FRIDAY Lev 25:39 "'If your brother has grown poor among you, and sells himself to you; you shall not make him to serve as a slave.

Lev 25:40 As a hired servant, and as a temporary resident, he shall be with you; he shall serve with you until the Year of Jubilee:

Lev 25:41 then he shall go out from you, he and his children with him, and shall return to his own family, and to the possession of his fathers.

Lev 25:42 For they are my servants, whom I brought out of the land of Egypt. They shall not be sold as slaves.

Lev 25:43 *You shall not rule over him with harshness, but shall fear your God.*

Lev 25:44 "'As for your male and your female slaves, whom you may have; of the nations that are around you, from them you may buy male and female slaves.

Lev 25:45 Moreover of the children of the aliens who live among you, of them you may buy, and of their families who are with you, which they have conceived in your land; and they will be your property.

Lev 25:46 You may make them an inheritance for your children after you, to hold for a possession; of them may you take your slaves forever; but over your brothers the children of Israel you shall not rule, one over another, with harshness.

Redeeming a Poor Man

<u>**SABBATH**</u> Lev 25:47 "'If an alien or temporary resident with you becomes rich, and your brother beside him has grown poor, and sells himself to the stranger or foreigner living among you, or to a member of the stranger's family;

Lev 25:48 after he is sold he may be redeemed. One of his brothers may redeem him;

Lev 25:49 or his uncle, or his uncle's son, may redeem him, or any who is a close relative to him of his family may redeem him; or if he has grown rich, he may redeem himself.

Lev 25:50 He shall reckon with him who bought him from the year that he sold himself to him to the Year of Jubilee. The price of his sale shall be according to the number of years; he shall be with him according to the time of a hired servant.

Lev 25:51 If there are yet many years, according to them he shall give back the price of his redemption out of the money that he was bought for.

Lev 25:52 If there remain but a few years to the year of jubilee, then he shall reckon with him; according to his years of service he shall give back the price of his redemption.

Lev 25:53 As a servant hired year by year shall he be with him. He shall not rule with harshness over him in your sight.

Lev 25:54 If he isn't redeemed by these means, then he shall be released in the Year of Jubilee, he, and his children with him.

Lev 25:55 *For to me the children of Israel are servants; they are my servants whom I brought out of the land of Egypt. I am YHWH your God.*

Blessings for Obedience

Lev 26:1 *"'You shall make for yourselves no idols, and you shall not raise up a carved image or a pillar, and you shall not place any figured stone in your land, to bow down to it; for I am YHWH your God.*

Lev 26:2 *"'You shall keep my Sabbaths, and have reverence for my sanctuary. I am YHWH.*

MY NOTES

~ EXTRA NOTES ~

CRYPTOGRAM — JEREMIAH 32:17

SCRAMBLE — 1 CORINTHIANS 7:23

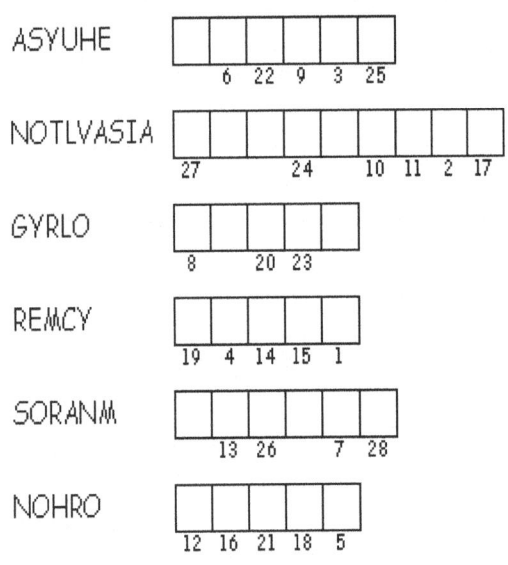

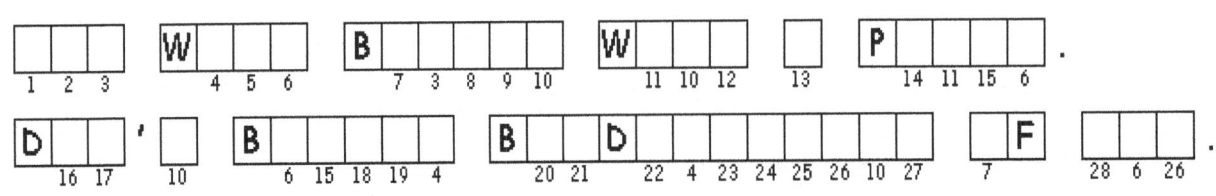

BECHUKOTAI
בְּחֻקֹּתַי
LEVITICUS

It Means: **In My Statutes**

Our Thirty-Third Torah Portion is called Bechukotai! בְּחֻקֹּתַי
Leviticus 26:3 – Leviticus 27:34

PROPHETS: Jeremiah 16:17-17:14; 23:1-40; 30:1-31:40; Ezekiel 37; Hosea 2; Zechariah 11:12-17
NEW TESTAMENT: Matthew 5:1-48; 7:1-29; 21:33-46; 23:1-24:2; 27:1-10; Luke 15; John 8:1-11; 14:15-21; 15:10-12; 2 Corinthians 6:14-18

MAKE A MARK

Each time you hear someone say one of the words below make a "/" beside the word. See how many marks you can get!

pride	
strength	
firstborn	
obedience	
father	
fruit	

FIRST FIND

~

If someone mentions a verse or scripture that is NOT in this Torah Portion, see if YOU can be the First to Find it!

BECHUKOTAI

```
R O H B A E M E G A T N I V D
R H X Y C D T E E U E V F F G
K U T Z R O E A K D I R T R F
V O N G Q A N S C O I O T U I
Z G G C N S R S O I Y R E I R
E G N N I E I T U L D R P T S
G C M N I R R M N M A E Z F T
A C O A O H C T U O P T D U B
D J A N H S S U S L C T I L O
N H U A F A A E M J T I I O R
O U E Z S E R E R S A I Y O N
B H W W F I S B S H I C P V N
T D R O W S L S A W T S O L U
C O M M A N D M E N T S E B Y
E T V P S S E N T N I A F D K
```

ABHOR
ABRAHAM
BONDAGE
COMMANDMENTS
CONFESS
CONSUMPTION
CONTRARY
DEDICATE
DESOLATION
FAINTNESS
FIRSTBORN
FRUITFUL
ISAAC
JACOB
MULTIPLY
PRIDE
SEASON
STRENGTH
SWORD
TERROR
THRESHING
UNCIRCUMSISED
VINTAGE
YOKE

Word Search Created by Torah Town

SUNDAY Lev 26:3 *"If you walk in my statutes, and keep my commandments, and do them;*

Lev 26:4 **then I will give you your rains in their season, and the land shall yield its increase, and the trees of the field shall yield their fruit.**

Lev 26:5 Your threshing shall reach to the vintage, and the vintage shall reach to the sowing time. You shall eat your bread to the full, and dwell in your land safely.

MONDAY Lev 26:6 "'I will give peace in the land, and you shall lie down, and no one will make you afraid. I will remove evil animals out of the land, neither shall the sword go through your land.

Lev 26:7 You shall chase your enemies, and they shall fall before you by the sword.

Lev 26:8 Five of you shall chase a hundred, and a hundred of you shall chase ten thousand; and your enemies shall fall before you by the sword.

Lev 26:9 **"'I will have respect for you, and make you fruitful, and multiply you, and will establish my covenant with you.**

TUESDAY Lev 26:10 You shall eat old store long kept, and you shall move out the old because of the new.

Lev 26:11 I will set my tent among you, and my soul won't abhor you.

Lev 26:12 *I will walk among you, and will be your God, and you will be my people.*

Lev 26:13 I am YHWH your God, who brought you out of the land of Egypt, that you should not be their slaves. I have broken the bars of your yoke, and made you go upright.

Punishment for Disobedience

Lev 26:14 *"'But if you will not listen to me, and will not do all these commandments;*

Lev 26:15 and if you shall reject my statutes, and if your soul abhors my ordinances, so that you will not do all my commandments, but break my covenant;

Lev 26:16 I also will do this to you: I will appoint terror over you, even consumption and fever, that shall consume the eyes, and make the soul to pine away. You will sow your seed in vain, for your enemies will eat it.

Lev 26:17 *I will set my face against you, and you will be struck before your enemies. Those who hate you will rule over you; and you will flee when no one pursues you.*

MY NOTES

Lev 26:18 "'If you in spite of these things will not listen to me, then I will chastise you seven times more for your sins.

Lev 26:19 I will break the pride of your power, and I will make your sky like iron, and your soil like brass.

Lev 26:20 Your strength will be spent in vain; for your land won't yield its increase, neither will the trees of the land yield their fruit.

Lev 26:21 *"**If you walk contrary to me, and won't listen to me, then I will bring seven times more plagues on you according to your sins.***

Lev 26:22 I will send the wild animals among you, which will rob you of your children, destroy your livestock, and make you few in number. Your roads will become desolate.

Lev 26:23 "'If by these things you won't be reformed to me, but will walk contrary to me;

Lev 26:24 then I will also walk contrary to you; and I will strike you, even I, seven times for your sins.

Lev 26:25 I will bring a sword upon you that will execute the vengeance of the covenant. You will be gathered together within your cities, and I will send the pestilence among you. You will be delivered into the hand of the enemy.

Lev 26:26 When I break your staff of bread, ten women shall bake your bread in one oven, and they shall deliver your bread again by weight. You shall eat, and not be satisfied.

Lev 26:27 "'If you in spite of this won't listen to me, but walk contrary to me;

Lev 26:28 then I will walk contrary to you in wrath. I will also chastise you seven times for your sins.

Lev 26:29 You will eat the flesh of your sons, and you will eat the flesh of your daughters.

Lev 26:30 I will destroy your high places, and cut down your incense altars, and cast your dead bodies upon the bodies of your idols; and my soul will abhor you.

Lev 26:31 I will lay your cities waste, and will bring your sanctuaries to desolation. I will not take delight in the sweet fragrance of your offerings.

Lev 26:32 I will bring the land into desolation; and your enemies that dwell therein will be astonished at it.

Lev 26:33 I will scatter you among the nations, and I will draw out the sword after you. Your land will be a desolation, and your cities shall be a waste.

Lev 26:34 Then the land will enjoy its Sabbaths as long as it lies desolate and you are in your enemies' land. Even then the land will rest and enjoy its Sabbaths.

Lev 26:35 As long as it lies desolate it shall have rest, even the rest which it didn't have in your Sabbaths, when you lived on it.

Lev 26:36 "'As for those of you who are left, I will send a faintness into their hearts in the lands of their enemies. The sound of a driven leaf will put them to flight; and they shall flee, as one flees from the sword. They will fall when no one pursues.

Lev 26:37 They will stumble over one another, as it were before the sword, when no one pursues. You will have no power to stand before your enemies.

Lev 26:38 You will perish among the nations. The land of your enemies will eat you up.

Lev 26:39 Those of you who are left will pine away in their iniquity in your enemies' lands; and also in the iniquities of their fathers they shall pine away with them.

Lev 26:40 ***"'If they confess their iniquity, and the iniquity of their fathers, in their trespass which they trespassed against me, and also that, because they walked contrary to me,***

Lev 26:41 I also walked contrary to them, and brought them into the land of their enemies; if then their uncircumcised heart is humbled, and they then accept the punishment of their iniquity;

Lev 26:42 then I will remember my covenant with Jacob; and also my covenant with Isaac, and also my covenant with Abraham; and I will remember the land.

Lev 26:43 The land also will be left by them, and will enjoy its Sabbaths while it lies desolate without them: and they will accept the punishment of their iniquity; because, even because they rejected my ordinances, and their soul abhorred my statutes.

Lev 26:44 Yet for all that, when they are in the land of their enemies, I will not reject them, neither will I abhor them, to destroy them utterly, and to break my covenant with them; for I am YHWH their God;

Lev 26:45 but I will for their sake remember the covenant of their ancestors, whom I brought out of the land of Egypt in the sight of the nations, that I might be their God. I am YHWH.'"

Lev 26:46 These are the statutes, ordinances and laws, which YHWH made between him and the children of Israel in Mount Sinai by Moses.

Laws About Vows

WEDNESDAY Lev 27:1 YHWH spoke to Moses, saying,

Lev 27:2 *"Speak to the children of Israel, and say to them, 'When a man consecrates a person to YHWH in a vow, according to your valuation,*

Lev 27:3 your valuation of a male from twenty years old even to sixty years old shall be fifty shekels of silver, after the shekel of the sanctuary.

Lev 27:4 If she is a female, then your valuation shall be thirty shekels.

Lev 27:5 If the person is from five years old even to twenty years old, then your valuation shall be for a male twenty shekels, and for a female ten shekels.

Lev 27:6 If the person is from a month old even to five years old, then your valuation shall be for a male five shekels of silver, and for a female your valuation shall be three shekels of silver.

Lev 27:7 If the person is from sixty years old and upward; if he is a male, then your valuation shall be fifteen shekels, and for a female ten shekels.

Lev 27:8 But if he is poorer than your valuation, then he shall be set before the priest, and the priest shall assign a value to him. The priest shall assign a value according to his ability to pay.

Lev 27:9 "'If it is an animal, of which men offer an offering to YHWH, all that any man gives of such to YHWH becomes holy.

Lev 27:10 He shall not alter it, nor change it, a good for a bad, or a bad for a good: and if he shall at all change animal for animal, then both it and that for which it is changed shall be holy.

Lev 27:11 If it is any unclean animal, of which they do not offer as an offering to YHWH, then he shall set the animal before the priest;

Lev 27:12 and the priest shall value it, whether it is good or bad. As you the priest values it, so shall it be.

Lev 27:13 But if he will indeed redeem it, then he shall add the fifth part of it to its valuation.

Lev 27:14 *"'When a man dedicates his house to be holy to YHWH, then the priest shall evaluate it, whether it is good or bad: as the priest shall evaluate it, so shall it stand.*

Lev 27:15 If he who dedicates it will redeem his house, then he shall add the fifth part of the money of your valuation to it, and it shall be his.

THURSDAY Lev 27:16 "'If a man dedicates to YHWH part of the field of his possession, then your valuation shall be according to the seed for it. The sowing of a homer of barley shall be valued at fifty shekels of silver.

Lev 27:17 If he dedicates his field from the Year of Jubilee, according to your valuation it shall stand.

Lev 27:18 But if he dedicates his field after the Jubilee, then the priest shall reckon to him the money according to the years that remain to the Year of Jubilee; and an abatement shall be made from your valuation.

Lev 27:19 If he who dedicated the field will indeed redeem it, then he shall add the fifth part of the money of your valuation to it, and it shall remain his.

Lev 27:20 If he will not redeem the field, or if he has sold the field to another man, it shall not be redeemed any more;

Lev 27:21 **but the field, when it goes out in the Jubilee, shall be holy to YHWH, as a devoted field. It shall be owned by the priests.**

FRIDAY Lev 27:22 "'If he dedicates a field to YHWH which he has bought, which is not of the field of his possession,

Lev 27:23 then the priest shall reckon to him the worth of your valuation up to the Year of Jubilee; and he shall give your valuation on that day, as a holy thing to YHWH.

Lev 27:24 In the Year of Jubilee the field shall return to him from whom it was bought, even to him to whom the possession of the land belongs.

Lev 27:25 All your valuations shall be according to the shekel of the sanctuary: twenty gerahs to the shekel.

Lev 27:26 **"'Only the firstborn among animals, which is made YHWH's firstborn, no man may dedicate; whether an ox or a sheep. It is YHWH's.**

Lev 27:27 If it is an unclean animal, then he shall buy it back according to your valuation, and shall add to it the fifth part of it; or if it isn't redeemed, then it shall be sold according to your valuation.

Lev 27:28 "'Notwithstanding, no devoted thing, that a man shall devote to YHWH of all that he has, whether of man or animal, or of the field of his possession, shall be sold or redeemed. Everything devoted to destruction is most holy to YHWH.

MY NOTES

SABBATH Lev 27:29 "'No one devoted, who shall be devoted from among men, shall be ransomed; he shall surely be put to death.

Lev 27:30 "'All the tithe of the land, whether of the seed of the land or of the fruit of the trees, is YHWH's. It is holy to YHWH.

Lev 27:31 **If a man redeems anything of his tithe, he shall add a fifth part to it.**

Lev 27:32 All the tithe of the herds or the flocks, whatever passes under the rod, the tenth shall be holy to YHWH.

Lev 27:33 He shall not search whether it is good or bad, neither shall he change it. If he changes it at all, then both it and that for which it is changed shall be holy. It shall not be redeemed.'"

Lev 27:34 These are the commandments which YHWH commanded Moses for the children of Israel on Mount Sinai.

MY NOTES

~ EXTRA NOTES ~

VERSE FIND – 2 CORINTHIANS 6:14

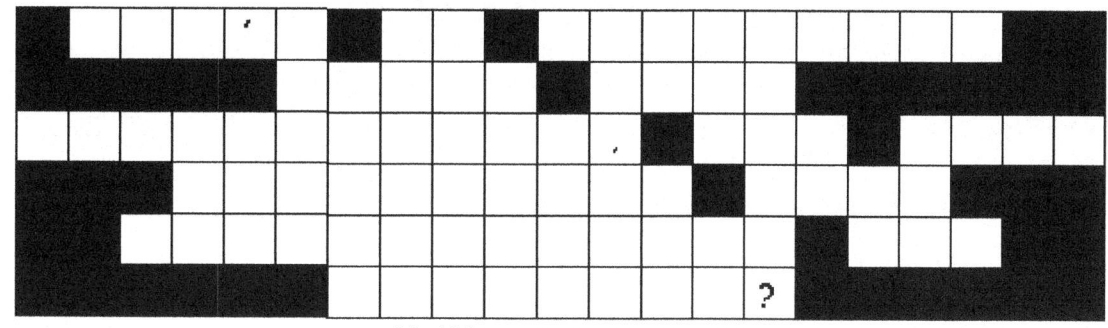

VERSE FIND 2 – JEREMIAH 30:3

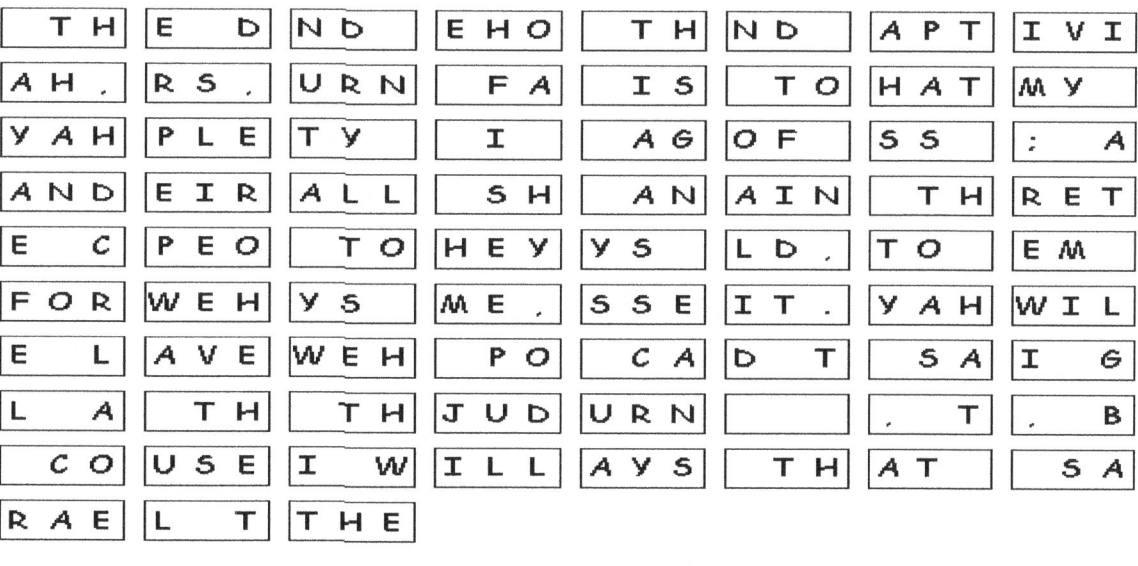

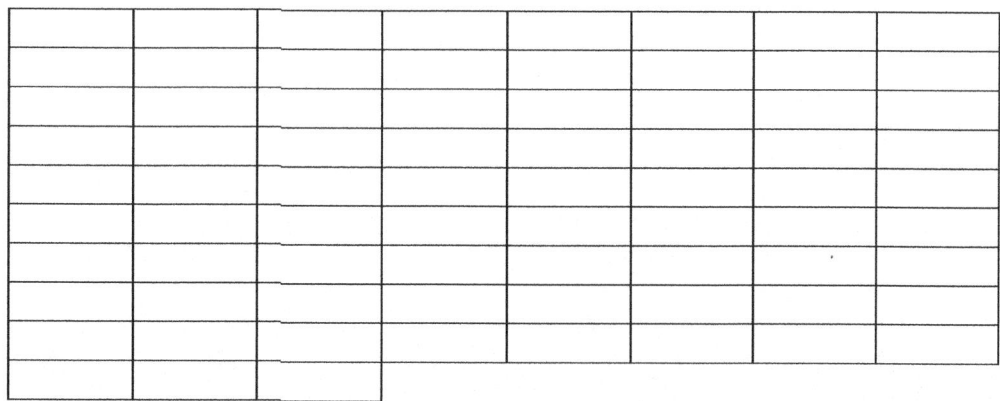

LEVITICUS
Four Great Lessons from the Book of Leviticus

* The Holiness of YHWH * The Necessity for Holy Living *
*The Great cost of Atonement *
* The Privilege And Responsibility of giving YHWH only our Best *

Why did YHWH require Sacrifices?
In the Moral Government of YHWH, physical and eternal death must be the penalty of Sin. (Gen, 2:17; Exe. 18:4)
"For the wages of Sin is Death, but the gift of YHWH is Eternal Life in Jesus Christ our Lord." (Rom. 6:23)
The fact that YHWH requires such a terrible punishment shows us just how terrible sin really is.

The Sacrifice of Yeshua
Yeshua (Jesus) was the perfect Son of God. He was the substitute that died in our place. Yeshua (Jesus) shed his blood to atone for our sin.
"How much more then will the Blood of Christ, who, through the eternal Spirit offered Himself unblemished toYHWH, cleanse our consciences from acts that lead to death, so that we may serve the Living God!"
(Heb. 9:14)

4 OFFERINGS

The Burnt Offering (Lev. 6) total and complete sacrifice.
Points to Yeshua's Complete offering of Himself.
"My Father, if it is possible, may this cup be taken away from me. Yet not as I will, but as You will." (Matt. 26:39)
During the Days of Yeshua's life on Earth, He offered up prayers and petitions with loud cries and tears to the One who could save Him from death, and He was heard because of His reverent submission. Although He was a Son, He learned obedience from what He suffered and, once made perfect, He became the Source of Eternal Salvation for all who obey Him. (Heb. 5:7-9)

The Grain Offering (Lev. 6) made into bread without yeast and burnt.
Points to Yeshua, His sinless life and work.
"Then Yeshua declared, "I am the Bread of Life. He who comes to Me will never go hungry, and he who believes in me will never go thirsty."" (John 6:35)

The Peace (Fellowship) Offering (Lev. 7)
Points to fellowship that believers have with YHWH through the sacrifice on the cross.
"Yeshua replied, :If anyone loves Me, he will Obey My Teaching. My Father will love him, and we will come to him and make our home with him." (John 14:23)

The Sin Offering (Lev. 7): Offered in repentance
Points to Yeshua's sacrifice that took our guilt and sin.
"Having therefore, brothers, boldness to enter into the holy place by the blood of Jesus, by the way which he dedicated for us, a new and living way, through the veil, that is to say, his flesh; and having a great priest over God's house, let's draw near with a true heart in fullness of faith, having our hearts sprinkled from an evil conscience, and having our body washed with pure water, let us hold fast the confession of our hope without wavering; for he who promised is faithful." (Heb. 10:19-23)

ALL OF SCRIPTURE POINTS TO
YESHUA HAMASHIACH

Made in the USA
Middletown, DE
24 March 2019